Lullaby
Knits

First published in the United Kingdom in 2013 by
Collins & Brown
10 Southcombe Street
London W14 0RA

An imprint of Anova Books Company Ltd

ISBN 978-1-90844-938-2

A CIP catalogue record for this book is
available from the British Library.

10 9 8 7 6 5 4 3 2 1

Reproduction by Mission, Hong Kong
Printed by 1010 Printing International Ltd, China

This book can be ordered direct from
the publisher at www.anovabooks.com

Lullaby Knits

Over 20 knitting patterns for 0–2 year olds

Vibe Ulrik Sondergaard

COLLINS & BROWN

Contents

Introduction

I am not sure I know anyone who doesn't find baby clothes cute and there is so much out there in the shops that it can sometimes be hard to compete as a knitter. Having said that, to give something that you have made yourself always seems just that bit more special, not least if the yarn is lovely and soft and the one to wear it is someone you care an awful lot about.

I was delighted when given the opportunity to make this book but also a bit daunted. There are quite a few practical things to consider when designing for babies and also, I had never designed for boys before. The compilation of these final pieces are a mixture of designs that are intended to be used for both boys and girls although a few are definitely mostly for girls. As in my previous book, Labour of Love, some projects are quite easy and others require more experience. Buttonholes are few and far between and mostly worked as a simple line of crochet. I had the intention to choose yarn consciously with regards to wear, tear and washing instructions but a few slipped in that did not meet all these criteria – simply because the yarn was too soft and luscious to resist!

I feel very honoured when someone tells me they have tried out a pattern from my first book and I hope, whether you are knitting for your own little new world citizen or your grandchild, a friend's baby or a nephew or a niece, that there is something here that you will find tempting enough to try out. The good thing about baby clothes is that that the pieces are all quite small, so even a challenging pattern is faster to finish than an adult's.

I hope this book will help spur you on – once you succeed with a proud result, you will never go back.

My warmest wishes and I hope you will enjoy your knitting,

Vibe U. Søndergaard

Sweaters

Easy Cable Sweater

If you work with lovely yarn, even the simplest cable will come out well. Worked in stocking stitch and a few cables, this is one for a beginner 'cable enthusiast' to try!

MEASUREMENTS

Size	3–6 mths	6–9 mths	9–12 mths	12–18 mths	18–24 mths
Finished chest measurement	48cm	51.5cm	55cm	58cm	61.5cm
Finished sleeve seam	11cm	14cm	15.5cm	17cm	18.5cm

YARN

2(2:3:3:3) x 50g balls of Rowan Baby Merino Silk DK in Zinc 681

MATERIALS

Pair of 3.5mm knitting needles
Cable needle
4 stitch holders
Tapestry needle

TENSION

20 sts and 28 rows to 10cm over st st using 3.5mm needles

Abbreviations

C12B – slip next 6 sts onto cable needle and hold at back of work, knit next 6 sts from left-hand needle, then knit 6 sts from cable needle.
C12F – slip next 6 sts onto cable needle and hold at front of work, knit next 6 sts from left-hand needle, then knit 6 sts from cable needle.
See also page 140

Back and front (both alike)

Cast on 58(62:66:70:74) sts.
Starting with a knit (RS) row, work 6(10:14:6:10) rows st st.
Next row: K5(7:9:11:13), C12F, k24, C12F, k5(7:9:11:13).
Work 11 rows st st.
Next row: K23(25:27:29:31), C12B, k23(25:27:29:31).
Work 9 rows st st.
Next row: K5(7:9:11:13), C12F, k24, C12F, k5(7:9:11:13).
Work 9 rows st st.
SIZES 12–18 AND 18–24 ONLY
Next row: K29(31), C12B, k29(31).
Work 11 rows st st.
Next row: K11(13), C12F, k24, C12F, k11(13).
Work 11 rows st st.
ALL SIZES
Shape raglan armholes
Next row: Cast off 2 sts (1 st on right-hand needle), k20(22:24:26:28), C12B, k to end of row.
56(60:64:68:72) sts
Next row: Cast off 2 sts, p to end of row.
54(58:62:66:70) sts
Next row: K3, ssk, k to last 5 sts, k2tog, k3.
52(56:60:64:68) sts
Next row: Purl.

Easy Cable Sweater

Rep last 2 rows, 9 times more. *34(38:42:46:50) sts*
Next row: K3, ssk, k6(8:10:12:14), C12B, k to last 5 sts, k2tog, k3. *32(36:40:44:48) sts*
Next row: Purl.
Work 6(6:10:14:14) rows st st, dec 1 st as set at each end of every alt row. *26(30:30:30:34) sts*
Leave sts on a stitch holder.

SLEEVE (MAKE TWO)

Cast on 28(30:30:34:34) sts.
Starting with a knit (RS) row, work in st st, inc 1 st at each end of every 8th row until there are 36(40:40:46:46) sts, ending with a purl (WS) row.
Work 4 more rows st st for sizes 9–12 and 18–24 only.
Shape raglan sleeve top
Cont in st st, casting off 2 sts at beg of next 2 rows. *32(36:36:42:42) sts*
Next row: K3, ssk, k to last 5 sts, k2tog, k3. *30(34:34:40:40) sts*
Next row: Purl.
Cont in patt as set by last 2 rows until there are 4(8:4:6:6) sts, ending with a WS row.
Leave sts on a stitch holder.

TO MAKE UP

Weave in loose ends.
Press the pieces following directions on the ball band.

Neckband
RS facing, slip sts from stitch holders onto needle in this order: back, sleeve, front, sleeve. *60(76:68:72:80) sts*
Starting with a k row, work 7 rows st st.
Cast off.

Sew up the raglans and neckband. Sew up the underarm and side seams from end of sleeve to lower edge of body.

Easy Cable Sweater

Bell Rib Sweater

A classic little jumper for the special little man in your life.
The pattern is a rib with a twist.

MEASUREMENTS

Size	3–6 mths	6–12 mths	12–18 mths	18–24 mths
Finished chest measurement	50cm	54cm	58cm	60cm
Finished sleeve seam	13cm	17.5cm	20cm	22cm

YARN

2(3:4:4) x 50g balls of Debbie Bliss Baby Cashmerino in Mist 340057

MATERIALS

Pair each of 3mm and 4mm knitting needles
Cable needle
3 stitch holders
Tapestry needle
8 x 12mm buttons
Sewing needle and thread

TENSION

22 sts and 26 rows to 10cm over bell rib patt using 4mm needles

ABBREVIATIONS

See page 140

BELL RIB PATTERN

(Worked over multiple of 4 sts + 2 sts)
Row 1 (WS): P2, [k2, p2] to end of row.
Row 2: K2, [p2, k2] to end of row.
Row 3: As row 1.
Row 4: As row 2.
Row 5: As row 1.
Row 6: K1, *slip next st onto cable needle and hold at front of work, p1, wyib skip next st, pass foll st over skipped st and then knit this st, knit st from cable needle, then purl skipped st; rep from * to last st, k1.
Row 7: K2, [p2, k2] to end of row.
Row 8: P2, [k2, p2] to end of row.
Row 9: As row 7.
Row 10: As row 8.
Row 11: As row 7.
Row 12: K1, skip next st, pass foll st over skipped st and then knit this st, then purl skipped st, [slip next st onto cable needle and hold at front of work, p1, wyib skip next st, pass foll st over skipped st and then knit this st, knit st from cable needle, then purl skipped st] to last 3 sts, slip next st onto cable needle and hold at front of work, p1, knit st from cable needle, k1.

BACK

Using 3mm needles, cast on 58(62:66:70) sts.
Row 1 (RS): [K1, p1] to end of row.
Rep row 1, 4 times more.
Change to 4mm needles.
Work 12 rows of bell rib patt 2(3:3:4) times.
Work 6 more rows in patt for size 12–18 only.
Shape raglan armholes
Keeping patt correct as set, cast off 2 sts at beg of next 2 rows. *54(58:62:66) sts*
Dec 1 st at each end of every alt row until there are 24(28:32:36) sts.
Leave sts on a stitch holder.

FRONT

Using 3mm needles, cast on 58(62:66:70) sts.
Row 1 (RS): [K1, p1] to end of row.
Rep row 1, 4 times more.
Change to 4mm needles.
Work 12 rows of bell rib patt 2(3:3:4) times.
Work 6 more rows in patt for size 12–18 only.
Shape raglan armholes
Keeping patt correct as set, cast off 4 sts at beg of next 2 rows. *50(54:58:62) sts*
Dec 1 st at each end of every alt row until there are 20(24:28:32) sts.
Next row (WS): [P1, k1] to end.
Rep last row 3 times more.
Cast off.

Bell Rib Sweater

SLEEVE (MAKE TWO)

Using 3mm needles, cast on 34(34:38:38) sts.
Row 1 (RS): [K1, p1] to end of row.
Rep row 1, 4 times more.
Change to 4mm needles.
Work 12 rows of bell rib patt 2(3:3:4) times, then work in patt for 6(6:0:6) more rows, and **at the same time** inc 1 st at each end of every 10th row. *40(42:46:46) sts*
Shape raglan sleeve top
Keeping patt correct as set, cast off 2 sts at beg of next 2 rows. *36(38:42:42) sts*
Dec 1 st at each end of every alt row until there are 6(8:12:12) sts.
Leave sts on a stitch holder.

JOINING BACK AND SLEEVES

RS facing, slip sts from stitch holders onto 4mm needle in this order: sleeve, back, sleeve. *36(44:56:60) sts*
Next row (RS): [K1, p1] to end of row.
Rep last row 3 times more.
Cast off.

To make up

Weave in loose ends.

Press the pieces following directions on the ball band.

Using 3mm needles and with RS facing, pick up 33 sts along one raglan of front piece. Work k1, p1 rib for 4 rows, then cast off. Repeat along second raglan of front piece.

Sew up the raglans on back piece. Sew up the underarm and side seams from end of sleeve to lower edge of body.

Sew on 4 buttons evenly spaced along the open raglan edge of each sleeve. You do not need to make buttonholes because the buttons used are quite small; simply push the buttons through the rib on the front raglans to close.

Bell Rib Sweater

Small Cable Sweater

For this sweater, all four pieces are knitted separately first and then joined at the armholes to avoid seams. A simple cable pattern that works for both boys and girls.

MEASUREMENTS

Size	0–3 mths
Finished chest measurement	50cm
Finished sleeve seam	12.5cm

YARN

2 x 50g balls of Debbie Bliss Baby Cashmerino in Slate 340009

MATERIALS

Pair each of 3mm and 4mm knitting needles
Long 4mm circular needle
Cable needle
4 stitch holders
Tapestry needle
4mm crochet hook
1 x 12mm button
Sewing needle and thread

TENSION

21 sts and 28 rows to 10cm over cable patt using 4mm needles

C2B – slip next 1 st onto cable needle and hold at back of work, knit next 1 st from left-hand needle, then knit 1 st from cable needle.

C2F – slip next 1 st onto cable needle and hold at front of work, knit next 1 st from left-hand needle, then knit 1 st from cable needle.

C3B – slip next 2 sts onto cable needle and hold at back of work, knit next 1 st from left-hand needle, then knit 2 sts from cable needle.

C3F – slip next 1 st onto cable needle and hold at front of work, knit next 2 sts from left-hand needle, then knit 1 st from cable needle.

C4B – slip next 3 sts onto cable needle and hold at back of work, knit next 1 st from left-hand needle, then knit 3 sts from cable needle.

C4F – slip next 1 st onto cable needle and hold at front of work, knit next 3 sts from left-hand needle, then knit 1 st from cable needle.

See also page 140

BACK AND FRONT (BOTH ALIKE)

Using 3mm needles, cast on 53 sts.
Row 1: [P1, k1] to last st, p1.
Row 2: [K1, p1] to last st, k1.
Row 3: As row 1.
Change to 4mm needles and beg cable patt as folls:
Row 4 (RS): P4, [k9, p3] 3 times, k9, p4.
Row 5: K4, [p9, k3] 3 times, p9, k4.
Row 6: P4, [C4B, k1, C4F, p3] 3 times, C4B, k1, C4F, p4.
Row 7: As row 5.
Rep rows 4–7, 8 times more.
Leaves sts on a stitch holder.

SLEEVE (MAKE TWO)

Using 3mm needles, cast on 29 sts.
Row 1 (RS): [P1, k1] to last st, k1.
Row 2: [K1, p1] to last st, k1.
Row 3: As row 1.
Change to 4mm needles and beg cable patt as folls:
Row 4: P4, k9, p3, k9, p4.
Row 5: K4, p9, k3, p9, k4.
Row 6: P4, C4B, k1, C4F, p3, C4B, k1, C4F, p4.
Row 7: As row 5.
Rep rows 4–7 twice more.
Row 16: P2, m1, p2, k9, p3, k9, p2, m1, p2. *31 sts*
Row 17: K5, p9, k3, p9, k5.

Row 18: P5, C4B, k1, C4F, p3, C4B, k1, C4F, p5.
Row 19: As row 17.
Row 20: P5, k9, p3, k9, p5.
Row 21: As row 17.
Row 22: As row 18.
Row 23: As row 17.
Rep rows 20–23, 3 times more.
Leave sts on a stitch holder.

JOINING THE PIECES

RS facing, slip sts from stitch holders onto 4mm circular needle in this order: sleeve, back, sleeve, front. *168 sts*
It is easier to use a long circular needle because of the number of sts, but continue to work in rows not in the round.
Rows 1–2: Work in cable patt as set across all sts (these should be 1st and 2nd cable patt rows).
Row 3 (RS): P1, p2tog, p1, [C4B, k1, C4F, p3] 4 times, p2tog, p1, [C4B, k1, C4F, p3] twice, p2tog, p4, [C4B, k1, C4F, p3] 4 times, p2tog, p4, C4B, k1, C4F, p3, C4B, k1, C4F, p1, p2tog, p2. 163 sts
Row 4 and all WS rows: Knit the purl sts and purl the knit sts of previous row.
Row 5: P3, [k9, p3] 4 times, p2tog, p3, [k9, p3] twice, p2tog, p3, [k9, p3] 4 times, p2tog, p3, k9, p3, k9, p1, p2tog, p1. *159 sts*
Row 7: P3, [C4B, k1, C4F, p3] 3 times, C4B, k1,

Small Cable Sweater

C4F, p2, p3tog, p2, C4B, k1, C4F, p3, C4B, k1,
C4F, p2, p3tog, p2, [C4B, k1, C4F, p3] 3 times,
C4B, k1, C4F, p2, p3tog, p2, [C4B, k1, C4F, p3]
twice. *153 sts*

Row 9: Work in cable patt as set, dec 1 st between
each sleeve and body piece, and dec 1 st at each
end of row. *148 sts*

Row 11: As row 9. *143 sts*

There should now be 3 purl sts between the
sleeves and body pieces and 1 purl st at each end
of row.

Row 13: P1, [k9, p1, p2tog] 11 times, k9, p1. *132 sts*

Row 15: Work in cable patt as set.

Row 17: Work in cable patt, dec 2 sts in each cable
as folls: k2, ssk, k1, k2tog, k2. *108 sts*

Row 19: Work in cable patt, now with 7 sts in
each cable as folls: C3B, k1, C3F.

Row 21: Work in cable patt as set.

Row 23: Work in cable patt as set, dec 1 st
between cables. *97 sts*

Row 25: Work in cable patt, dec 2 sts in each
cable as folls: k1, ssk, k1, k2tog, k1. *73 sts*

Row 27: Work in cable patt, now with 5 sts in
each cable as folls: C2B, k1, C2F.

Row 28: As row 4.

Change to 3mm needles.

Row 29: [P1, k1] twice, p1, [sk2po, p1, k1, p1] 3
times, [k1, p1] 9 times, [sk2po, p1, k1, p1] 5 times,
k1, p1. *57 sts*

Row 30: [K1, p1] to last st, k1.

Cast off.

TO MAKE UP

Weave in loose ends.
Press the piece following directions on the
ball band.
Sew up the underarm and side seams from end
of sleeve to lower edge of body. Sew the front
left shoulder seam to about 7cm up from the
underarm, leaving the top open.
Work a simple crochet edging (such as double
crochet) along both of the open shoulders,
making a small chain loop for a buttonhole at the
top of the front edge. Sew a button onto the other
edge to match.

Small Cable Sweater

Little Tree Sweater

This sweater features a simple tree motif and would make a lovely little treat for either a boy or a girl.

MEASUREMENTS

Size	3–6 mths	6–9 mths	9–12 mths
Finished chest measurement	49cm	53cm	57.5cm
Finished sleeve seam	13.5cm	16.5cm	18cm

YARN

3(3:4) x 50g balls of Debbie Bliss Bella in Camel 16005

MATERIALS

Pair of 3.5mm knitting needles
Cable needle
4 stitch holders
Tapestry needle
3.5mm crochet hook
3 x 12mm buttons
Sewing needle and thread

TENSION

18 sts and 26 rows to 10cm over reverse st st using 3.5mm needles

ABBREVIATIONS

C2B – slip next 1 st onto cable needle and hold at back of work, knit next 1 st from left-hand needle, then purl 1 st from cable needle.

C2F – slip next 1 st onto cable needle and hold at front of work, purl next 1 st from left-hand needle, then knit 1 st from cable needle.

C4B – slip next 2 sts onto cable needle and hold at back of work, knit next 2 sts from left-hand needle, then purl 2 sts from cable needle.

C4F – slip next 2 sts onto cable needle and hold at front of work, purl next 2 sts from left-hand needle, then knit 2 sts from cable needle.

C2Btog – slip next 1 st onto cable needle and hold at back of work, knit next 1 st from left-hand needle, then slip cable st back onto left-hand needle and knit next 2 sts together.

C2Ftog – with yarn in back slip next 1 st onto cable needle and hold at front of work, knit next 2 sts together from left-hand needle, then knit 1 st from cable needle.

MB – make bobble: (k1, p1, k1, p1) all into next st, turn, p4, turn, k4, pass 2nd, 3rd and 4th sts over last st on right-hand needle.

See also page 140

BACK

Cast on 44(48:52) sts.
Rows 1–8: Knit.
Starting with a purl (RS) row, work 28(32:36) rows reverse st st.
Shape raglan armholes
Cont in reverse st st, casting off 1 st at beg of next 2 rows. *42(46:50) sts*
Dec 1 st at each end of next and every alt row until there are 22(24:26) sts.
Leave sts on a stitch holder.

FRONT

Cast on 44(48:52) sts.
Rows 1–8: Knit.
Row 9 (RS): P19(21:23), k6, p19(21:23).
Row 10: K19(21:23), p6, k19(21:23).
Rep rows 9–10, 5(7:9) times more.
Row 21(25:29): P19(21:23), k1, m1, k4, m1, k1, p19(21:23). *46(50:54) sts*
Row 22(26:30) and all WS rows: Knit the purl sts, purl the knit sts and knit the bobble sts of previous row.
Row 23(27:31): P19(21:23), k1, m1, k6, m1, k1, p19(21;23). *48(52:56) sts*
Row 25(29:33): P17(19:21), C4B, k6, C4F, p17(19:21).

Little Tree Sweater

Row 27(31:35): P15(17:19), C4B, p2, k1, m1, k4, m1, k1, p2, C4F, p15(17:19). *50(54:58) sts*

Row 29(33:37): P13(15:17), C4B, p4, k1, m1, k6, m1, k1, p4, C4F, p13(15:17). *52(56:60) sts*

Row 31(35:39): P11(13:15), C4B, p4, C4B, k6, C4F, p4, C4F, p11(13:15).

Row 33(37:41): P11(13:15), k2, p4, C4B, p2, k6, p2, C4F, p4, k2, p11(13:15).

Row 35(39:43): P10(12:14), C2Btog, p2, C4B, p4, k6, p4, C4F, p2, C2Ftog, p10(12:14). *50(54:58) sts*

Shape raglan armholes

Row 37(41:45): Cast off 1 st, p8(10:12) including st used to cast off, C2B, MB, p2, k2, p4, C4B, k2, C4F, p4, k2, p2, MB, C2F, p9(11:13). *49(53:57) sts*

Row 38(42:46): Cast off 1 st, then work as set for WS rows. *48(52:56) sts*

Row 39(43:47): P7(9:11), C2B, p3, C2Btog, p2, C4B, p2, k2, p2, C4F, p2, C2Ftog, p3, C2F, p7(9:11). *46(50:54) sts*

Row 40(44:48) and all WS rows: Work as set, dec 1 st at each end of this and all foll WS rows.

Row 41(45:49): P6(8:10), MB, p3, C2B, MB, p2, k2, p4, k2, p4, k2, p2, MB, C2F, p3, MB, p6(8:10).

Row 43(47:51): P8(10:12), C2B, p3, C2Btog, p4, k2, p4, C2Ftog, p3, C2F, p8(10:12). *40(44:48) sts*

Row 45(49:53): P7(9:11), MB, p3, C2B, MB, p3, C2B, C2F, p3, MB, C2F, p3, MB, p7(9:11). *38(42:46) sts*

Row 47(51:55): P9(11:13), C2B, p4, C2B, p2, C2F, p4, C2F, p9(11:13). *36(40:44) sts*
Row 49(53:57): P8(10:12), MB, p4, C2B, p4, C2F, p4, MB, p8(10:12). *34(38:42) sts*
Row 51(55:59): P12(14:16), MB, p6, MB, p12(14:16). *32(36:40) sts*
Row 53(57:61): Purl.
Row 55(59:63): Purl, dec 1 st at each end of row. *26(30:34) sts*
Work 2(4:6) rows in patt as set, dec 1 st at each end of every alt row. *24(26:28) sts*
Leave sts on a stitch holder.

SLEEVE (MAKE TWO)

Cast on 24(28:30) sts.
Rows 1–8: Knit.
Starting with a purl (RS) row, work in reverse st st, inc 1 st at each end of every 6th row until there are 34(40:44) sts.

Shape raglan sleeve top
Cast off 1 st at beg of next 2 rows. *32(38:42) sts*
Dec 1 st at each end of next and every alt row until there are 12(16:18) sts.
Leave sts on a stitch holder.

Weave in loose ends.
Steam the pieces following directions on the ball band.

Neckband
RS facing, slip sts from stitch holders onto needle in this order: sleeve, back, sleeve, front. *70(82:90) sts*
Next row (RS): [K2, k2tog] 3 times, k0(2:4), [k2tog, k2] 3 times, k2, k2tog, k4(8:10), k2tog, k2, [k2, k2tog] twice, k6(8:10), [k2tog, k2] twice, k2, k2tog, k4(8:10), k2tog, k2. *56(68:76) sts*
Knit 5 rows.
Cast off.

Sew up the raglans but leave the front left raglan open from the neck to a few centimetres above the underarm.
Sew up the underarm and side seams from end of sleeve to lower edge of body.
Work a simple crochet edging (such as double crochet) along both of the open raglan edges, making 3 small evenly spaced chain loops for buttonholes on the front edge. Sew buttons onto the other edge to match.

Little Tree Sweater

Cable and Daisy Stitch Sweater

This sweater pattern lends itself to a yarn with good stitch definition because of its textured nature. It can be worn with the button at the front or back as preferred.

MEASUREMENTS

Size	6–12 mths	12–18 mths	18–24 mths
Finished chest measurement	50cm	58cm	66cm
Finished sleeve seam	16cm	18cm	20cm

YARN

5(5:6) x 50g balls of Debbie Bliss Eco Aran in Rice Cake 32631

MATERIALS

Pair each of 3mm, 4mm and 5mm knitting needles
Cable needle
Tapestry needle
5mm crochet hook
2 x 15mm buttons
Sewing needle and thread

TENSION

18 sts and 22 rows to 10cm over central cable patt using 4mm needles

C3B – slip next 2 sts onto cable needle and hold at back of work, knit next 1 st from left-hand needle, then knit 2 sts from cable needle.
C3F – slip next 1 st onto cable needle and hold at front of work, knit next 2 sts from left-hand needle, then knit 1 st from cable needle.
MK – make knot: p3tog leaving sts on needle, yo, then purl the same sts together again.
See also page 140

BACK AND FRONT (BOTH ALIKE)

Using 3mm needles, cast on 47(55:63) sts.
Row 1 (RS): [K1, p1] to last st, k1.
Row 2: [P1, k1] to last st, p1.
Change to 4mm needles.
Row 3: K12(12:16), [C3B, k1, C3F, p1] 2(3:3) times, C3B, k1, C3F, k12(12:16).
Row 4: [K1, MK] 3(3:4) times, [p7, k1] 2(3:3) times, p7, [k1, MK] 3(3:4) times.
Row 5: As row 3.
Row 6: K1, p1, [k1, MK] 2(2:3) times, k1, p8, [k1, p7] 2(3:3) times, k1, p1, [k1, MK] 2(2:3) times, k1, p1.
Rows 3–6 form central cable panel with daisy (knot) stitch at side edges.
Rep rows 3–6 until work measures 16(18:20)cm from cast-on edge, ending with a row 6.

Shape raglan armholes

Next row: Cast off 2 sts, patt 21(25:29) sts including st used to cast off, inc 1, patt to end of row. *46(54:62) sts*

Next row: Cast off 2 sts, work daisy patt as established (row 4) **across all sts** to end of row. *44(52:60) sts*

Cont in daisy patt as set, dec 1 st at each end of next and every alt (RS) row for 10 rows. *34(42:50) sts*

Cast off.

Sleeve (make two)

Using 3mm needles, cast on 31(31:31) sts.

Row 1 (RS): [K1, p1] to last st, k1.

Row 2: [P1, k1] to last st, p1.

Change to 4mm needles.

Row 3: K8, C3B, k1, C3F, p1, C3B, k1, C3F, k8.

Row 4: [K1, MK] twice, p7, k1, p7, [k1, MK] twice.

Row 5: K8, C3B, k1, C3F, p1, C3B, k1, C3F, k8.

Row 6: K1, p1, k1, MK, k1, p8, k1, p9, k1, MK, k1, p1.

Rows 3–6 form central cable panel with daisy (knot) stitch at side edges.

Inc and work into daisy patt 1 st at each end of next and every foll 10th row until there are 37(39:39) sts.

Cont without shaping until work measures 16(18:20)cm, ending with a row 6.

Shape raglan sleeve top

Next row (RS): Cast off 2 sts, patt 16(17:17) sts including st used to cast off, inc 1, patt to end of row. *36(38:38) sts*

Next row: Cast off 2 sts, work daisy patt as established (row 4) **across all sts** to end of row. *34(36:36) sts*

Cont in daisy patt as set, dec 1 st at each end of next and every alt (RS) row for 10 rows. *24(26:26) sts*

Cast off.

Neckband

Sew up the pieces along the raglan seams.

Using 5mm needles, cast on 15 sts.

Row 1: Purl.

Row 2 (RS): C3B, k1, C3F, p1, C3B, k1, C3F.

Row 3: P7, k1, p7.

Row 4: C3B, k1, C3F, p1, C3B, k1, C3F.

Row 5: P7, k1, turn.

Row 6: P1, C3B, k1, C3F (when working the first purl stitch, purl it together with a loop from the previous row so as not to leave a gap between sts).

Row 7: P7, k1, p7.

Rep rows 2–7 until longest edge fits around neckline.

Cast off on the WS.

Mini Matilda Sweater

Weave in loose ends.

Press the pieces following directions on the ball band.

Pin the neckband around the neckline, beginning and ending at the front left raglan seam. Sew the neckband in place.

Sew up the underarm and side seams from end of sleeve to lower edge of body.

Work a simple crochet edging (such as double crochet) along both ends of the neckband, making 2 small chain loops for buttonholes on the front edge. Sew buttons onto the other edge to match.

Mini Matilda Sweater

Straight Neck Cable Sweater

A few cables and a pretty coloured yarn can go a long way to make a lovely sweater. This one requires little shaping for the front and back, which makes it even easier to knit.

MEASUREMENTS

Size	6–9 mths	9–12 mths	12–18 mths	18–24 mths
Finished chest measurement	50cm	56cm	62cm	68cm
Finished sleeve seam	13cm	13cm	16cm	18.5cm

YARN

3(3:4:4) x 50g balls of Debbie Bliss Baby Cashmerino in Duck Egg 340026

MATERIALS

Pair each of 3mm and 3.5mm knitting needles
Cable needle
Tapestry needle

TENSION

20 sts and 30 rows to 10cm over st st using 3.5mm needles

C6B – slip next 3 sts onto cable needle and hold at back of work, knit next 3 sts from left-hand needle, then knit 3 sts from cable needle.
C6F – slip next 3 sts onto cable needle and hold at front of work, knit next 3 sts from left-hand needle, then knit 3 sts from cable needle.
C8B – slip next 4 sts onto cable needle and hold at back of work, knit next 4 sts from left-hand needle, then knit 4 sts from cable needle.
C8F – slip next 4 sts onto cable needle and hold at front of work, knit next 4 sts from left-hand needle, then knit 4 sts from cable needle.
See also page 140

BACK AND FRONT (BOTH ALIKE)

Using 3mm needles, cast on 68(74:80:86) sts.
Row 1 (RS): [K2, p1] to last 2 sts, k2.
Row 2: [P2, k1] to last 2 sts, p2.
Rep rows 1–2, 4 times more.
Change to 3.5mm needles.
Row 11: P3(4:5:6), k13, p1(2:3:4), k8, p1(2:3:4), k16, p1(2:3:4), k8, p1(2:3:4), k13, p3(4:5:6).
Row 12 and all WS rows: Purl the knit sts and knit the purl sts of previous row.
Row 13: P3(4:5:6), C6B, k1, C6F, p1(2:3:4), C8B, p1(2:3:4), C8B, C8F, p1(2:3:4), C8F, p1(2:3:4),

Straight Neck Cable Sweater

C6B, k1, C6F, p3(4:5:6).

Row 15: As row 11.

Row 17: As row 11.

Row 19: P3(4:5:6), C6B, k1, C6F, p1(2:3:4), C8B, p1(2:3:4), C8F, C8B, p1(2:3:4), C8F, p1(2:3:4), C6B, k1, C6F, p3(4:5:6).

Row 21: As row 11.

Row 23: As row 11.

Rep rows 11–23 until work measures 14(16:18:20)cm from cast-on edge.

Shape armholes

Keeping patt correct as set, cast off 2 sts at beg of next 2 rows. *64(70:76:82) sts*

Cont in patt as set for another 6(7:8:9)cm, ending with a WS row.

Change to 3mm needles.

Next row (RS): K1, k2tog, [p1, k2] to last 4 sts, p1, k2tog, k1. *62(68:74:80) sts*

Next row: [P2, k1] to last 2 sts, p2.

Next row: [K2, p1] to last 2 sts, k2.

Rep last 2 rows, 3 times more.

Cast off.

SLEEVE (MAKE TWO)

Using 3mm needles, cast on 29(29:32:35) sts.

Row 1 (RS): [K2, p1] to last 2 sts, k2.

Row 2: [P2, k1] to last 2 sts, p2.

Rep rows 1–2, 3 times more, inc 1 st at each end

of last row. *31(31:34:37) sts*

Change to 3.5mm needles.

Starting with a k row, work in st st, inc 1 st at each end of every 8th row until there are 39(39:44:49) sts.

Shape sleeve top

Keeping patt correct as set, cast off 2 sts at beg of next 2 rows. *35(35:40:45) sts*

Dec 1 st at each end of next and every alt row for 6 rows. *29(29:34:39) sts*

Dec 1 st at each end of next and every foll row until there are 11(11:12:15) sts.

Cast off.

To make up

Weave in loose ends.

Steam the pieces following directions on the ball band.

Sew up the shoulder seams for about 4–5cm, making sure that the opening is big enough for the head to go through.

Sew the sleeves into the armholes. Sew up the underarm and side seams from end of sleeve to lower edge of body, leaving rib section at bottom of body open to form side slits.

Straight Neck Cable Sweater

Slip Stitch Sweater

The texture of this sweater is not as complicated as it might look. The repeated 'stripes' make a lovely simple feature.

MEASUREMENTS

Size	3–6 mths	6–9 mths	9–12 mths	12–18 mths	18–24 mths
Finished chest measurement	46cm	49cm	54cm	57cm	60cm
Finished sleeve seam	15cm	15cm	15cm	19cm	23cm

YARN

3(3:3:3:4) x 50g balls of Debbie Bliss Baby Cashmerino in Taupe 340049

MATERIALS

Pair each of 3mm and 4mm knitting needles
Long 4mm circular needle
Cable needle
4 stitch holders
Tapestry needle
4 x 12mm buttons
Sewing needle and thread

TENSION

22 sts and 28 rows to 10cm over patt using 4mm needles

ABBREVIATIONS

See page 140

SLIP STITCH PATTERN

(Worked over multiple of 3 sts)
Row 1 (RS): Knit.
Row 2: Purl.
Row 3: K2, [slip 1 wyib, k2] to last st, k1.
Row 4: P3, [slip 1 wyif, p2] to end of row.
Row 5: K2, [slip drop st onto cable needle and hold at front of work, k2, knit st from cable needle] to last st, k1.
Row 6: Purl.
Row 7: K2, [yo, k2tog, k1] to last st, k1.
Row 8: Purl.
Row 9: K4, [slip 1 wyib, k2] to last 2 sts, slip 1 wyib, k1.
Row 10: P1, [slip 1 wyif, p2] to last 2 sts, p2.
Row 11: K2, [slip 2 sts onto cable needle and hold at back of work, k1 (the slip stitch), knit 2 sts from cable needle] to last st, k1.
Row 12: Purl.

Back and Front (both alike)

Using 3mm needles, cast on 51(54:60:63:66) sts.
Row 1 (RS): [K1, p1] to last 1(0:0:1:0) sts,
k1(0:0:1:0).
Row 2: P1(0:0:1:0), [k1, p1] to end of row.
Rep rows 1–2 once more.
Change to 4mm needles.
Row 5: Knit.
Row 6: Purl.
Work 12 rows of slip stitch patt 3(3:3:4:4) times.
Leave sts on a stitch holder.

Sleeve (make two)

Using 3mm needles, cast on 30(30:33:33:36) sts.
Row 1 (RS): [K1, p1] to last 0(0:1:1:0) sts,
k0(0:1:1:0).
Row 2: P0(0:1:1:0), [k1, p1] to end of row.
Rep rows 1–2 once more.
Change to 4mm needles.
Row 5: Knit.
Row 6: Purl.
Work 12 rows of slip stitch patt 3(3:3:4:5) times,
and **at the same time** inc 1 st at each end of first
row of each patt repeat; **also at the same time**, for
size 12–18 only inc 1 st on last row of final patt
repeat and for size 18–24 only inc 1 st at each end
of last row of final patt repeat.

Work should measure about 15(15:15:19:23)cm
from cast-on edge. *36(36:39:42:48) sts*
Leave sts on a stitch holder.

Joining the pieces

The front is now split into two parts in order to
make the opening at the centre.
RS facing, slip sts from stitch holders onto 4mm
circular needle in this order: 25(26:29:31:32) sts of
left front, sleeve, back, sleeve, rem 26(28:31:32:34)
sts of right front. *174(180:198:210:228) sts*
It is easier to use a long circular needle because of
the number of sts, but continue to work in rows
not in the round.
Your starting point will now be the right front
with RS facing.
Dec 2 sts at each side of front and back and dec
1 st at each side of sleeves as folls:
Row 1 (RS): K22(24:27:28:30), k3tog, k2, ssk,
k30(30:33:36:42), k2tog, k2, sk2po,
k43(46:52:55:58), k3tog, k2, ssk,
k30(30:33:36:42), k2tog, k2, sk2po,
k21(22:25:27:28), cast on 4 sts.
166(172:190:202:220) sts
Row 2: Purl, inc 1 st at end of row.
167(173:191:203:221) sts
Row 3: K1 for edge st, work in slip stitch patt
(starting with a row 3) to last 4 sts, [p1, k1] twice.

Slip Stitch Sweater

Cont in patt for one whole patt repeat (12 rows), working edge st in st st and keeping front edge rib correct.

Next row: K4(7:4:4:7), [sk2po, k9] 13(13:15:16:17) times, k3(6:3:3:6), [p1, k1] twice. *141(147:161:171:187) sts*

Next row: Purl.

With 2(2:1:2:0) edge sts at beg of RS rows only, work in slip stitch patt (starting with a row 3) to last 4 sts, [p1, k1] twice. Cont in patt for one whole patt repeat.

Next row: K3(2:3:2:9), [sk2po, k3] 22(23:25:27:28) times, k2(1:2:1:4), [k2tog] 0(1:1:1:1) times, [p1, k1] twice. *97(100:110:116:130) sts*

Next row: Purl.

With 0(0:1:1:0) edge sts at beg of RS rows only, work in slip stitch patt (starting with a row 3) to last 4 sts, [p1, k1] twice. Cont in patt for one whole patt repeat.

SIZE 3–6 ONLY

Next row: K4, ssk, [k2, ssk] 21 times, k3, [p1, k1] twice. *75 sts*

Next row: [P1, k1] twice, p to end of row.

Next row: K3, ssk, [k3, ssk] 13 times, k1, [p1, k1] twice. *61 sts*

SIZE 6–9 ONLY

Next row: K2, ssk, [k3, ssk] 18 times, k2, [p1, k1] twice. *81 sts*

Next row: [P1, k1] twice, p to end of row.

Next row: K1, ssk, [k2, ssk] 18 times, ssk, [p1, k1] twice. *61 sts*

SIZE 9–12 ONLY

Next row: K2, ssk, [k3, ssk] 20 times, k2, [p1, k1] twice. *89 sts*

Next row: [P1, k1] twice, p to end of row.

Next row: K1, ssk, [k2, ssk] 20 times, ssk, [p1, k1] twice. *67 sts*

SIZE 12–18 ONLY

Next row: K7, [k3, sk2po] 17 times, k3, [p1, k1] twice. *82 sts*

Next row: [P1, k1] twice, p to end of row.

Next row: K1, sk2po, [k2, ssk] 18 times, ssk, [p1, k1] twice. *61 sts*

SIZE 18–24 ONLY

Next row: K6, sk2po, [k3, sk2po] 19 times, k3, [p1, k1] twice. *90 sts*

Next row: [P1, k1] twice, p to end of row.

Next row: K5, sk2po, [k5, sk2po] 9 times, k4, ssk, [p1, k1] twice. *69 sts*

ALL SIZES

Change to 3mm needles.

Next row: Purl.

Next row: [K1, p1] to last st, k1.

Next row: [P1, k1] to last st, p1.

Rep last 2 rows once more.

Cast off.

Slip Stitch Sweater

TO MAKE UP

Weave in loose ends.
Steam the piece following directions on the ball band.
Sew lower edge of cast-on sts for button band behind right front edge.
Sew up the underarm and side seams from end of sleeve to lower edge of body.
Sew 4 buttons onto the button band, one at the neck and another by each of the three pattern repeats so that the 'yo' in the pattern acts as a buttonhole. You do not need to make a buttonhole at the neck because the buttons used are quite small; simply push the button through the rib to close.

Cardigans & Jackets

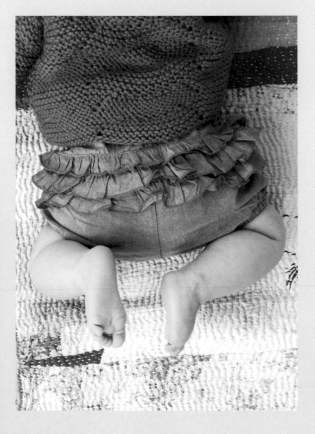

Lace Cardigan

A cardigan in simple lace and stocking stitch that works for both girls and boys. All pieces are joined at the top to avoid seams in the lace, then decreased in the end.

MEASUREMENTS

Size	3–6 mths	6–9 mths	9–12 mths	12–18 mths	18–24 mths
Finished chest measurement	43cm	49cm	55cm	61cm	67cm
Finished sleeve seam	12cm	12cm	16cm	17cm	20cm

YARN

2(2:2:3:4) x 50g balls of Rowan Baby Merino Silk DK in Rose 678 or Teal 677

MATERIALS

Pair each of 3mm and 3.5mm knitting needles
Long 3.5mm circular needle (optional)
5 stitch holders
Tapestry needle
4 or 5 x 12mm buttons
Sewing needle and thread

TENSION

20 sts and 28 rows to 10cm over st st using 3.5mm needles

ABBREVIATIONS

See page 140

BACK

Using 3mm needles, cast on 43(49:55:61:67) sts.
Row 1 (RS): [K1, p1] to last st, k1.
Row 2: [P1, k1] to last st, p1.
Rep rows 1–2 once more.
Change to 3.5mm needles.
Starting with a k row, work in st st for 8(12:16:20:24) rows.
Next row: K6, [p1, k5] to last st, k1.
Next row: K1, [p5, k1] to end of row.
Next row: K1, [yo, ssk, p1, k2tog, yo, k1] to end of row.
Next row: K1, p2, [k1, p5] to last 4 sts, k1, p2, k1.
Next row: K3, [p1, k5] to last 4 sts, p1, k3.
Next row: K1, p2, [k1, p5] to last 4 sts, k1, p2, k1.
Next row: K1, [k2tog, yo, k1, yo, ssk, p1] to last 6 sts, k2tog, yo, k1, yo, ssk, k1.
Next row: K1, [p5, k1] to end of row.
Rep last 8 rows once more.
Work 4 rows st st.
Shape armholes
Next row: Cast off 2(1:1:1:2) sts, k to end of row. *41(48:54:60:65) sts*
Next row: Cast off 2(1:1:1:2) sts, p to end of row. *39(47:53:59:63) sts*
Cont in st st, dec 1 st at each end of next and every alt row for 6 rows. *33(41:47:53:57) sts*
Work another 2 rows st st without shaping for sizes 12–18 and 18–24 only.
Leave sts on a stitch holder.

LEFT FRONT

Note: Sizes 3–6, 9–12 and 18–24 have 6 sts of rib at centre front edge.
Sizes 6–9 and 12–18 have 4 sts of rib at centre front edge.
Using 3mm needles, cast on 25(29:31:35:37) sts.
Row 1 (RS): [K1, p1] to last st, k1.
Row 2: [P1, k1] to last st, p1.
Rep rows 1–2 once more.
Change to 3.5mm needles.
Row 5: K to last 6(4:6:4:6) sts, [p1, k1] 3(2:3:2:3) times.
Row 6: [P1, k1] 3(2:3:2:3) times, p to end of row.
Starting with a k row, work in st st while maintaining centre rib for 6(10:14:18:22) rows.
Next row: K6, [p1, k5] to last 6(4:6:4:6) sts, [p1, k1] to end of row.
Next row: [P1, k1] 3(2:3:2:3) times, k1, [p5, k1] to end of row.
Next row: K1, [yo, ssk, p1, k2tog, yo, k1] to last 6(4:6:4:6) sts, [p1, k1] to end of row.
Next row: [P1, k1] 3(2:3:2:3) times, k1, p2, [k1, p5] to last 4 sts, k1, p2, k1.
Next row: K3, [p1, k5] to last 10(8:10:8:10) sts, p1, k3, [p1, k1] 3(2:3:2:3) times.
Next row: [P1, k1] 3(2:3:2:3) times, k1, p2, [k1, p5] to last 4 sts, k1, p2, k1.
Next row: K1, [k2tog, yo, k1, yo, ssk, p1] to last 12(10:12:10:12) sts, k2tog, yo, k1, yo, ssk, k1, [p1, k1] 3(2:3:2:3) times.

Lace Cardigan

Next row: [P1, k1] 3(2:3:2:3) times, k1, [p5, k1] to end of row.

Rep last 8 rows once more.

Maintaining centre rib, work 4 rows st st.

Shape armhole

Next row (RS): Cast off 1 st, k to end of row, maintaining centre rib. *24(28:30:34:36) sts*

Next row: Purl, maintaining centre rib.

Cont in st st maintaining centre rib, dec 1 st at armhole edge of next and every alt row for 6 rows. *21(25:27:31:33) sts*

Work 2 more rows st st without shaping for sizes 12–18 and 18–24 only.

Leave sts on a stitch holder.

RIGHT FRONT

Note: Sizes 3–6, 9–12 and 18–24 have 6 sts of rib at centre front edge.

Sizes 6–9 and 12–18 have 4 sts of rib at centre front edge.

Using 3mm needles, cast on 25(29:31:35:37) sts.

Row 1 (RS): [K1, p1] to last st, k1.

Row 2: [P1, k1] to last st, p1.

Rep rows 1–2 once more.

Change to 3.5mm needles.

Row 5: [K1, p1] 3(2:3:2:3) times, k to end of row.

Row 6: P to last 6(4:6:4:6) sts, [k1, p1] to end of row.

Lace Cardigan

Starting with a k row, work in st st while
maintaining centre rib for 6(10:14:18:22) rows.
Next row: [K1, p1] 3(2:3:2:3) times, k6, [p1, k5]
to last st, k1.
Next row: K1, [p5, k1] to last 6(4:6:4:6) sts,
[k1, p1] 3(2:3:2:3) times.
Next row: [K1, p1] 3(2:3:2:3) times, k1, [yo, ssk,
p1, k2tog, yo, k1] to end of row.
Next row: K1, p2, [k1, p5] to last 10(8:10:8:10) sts,
k1, p2, k1, [k1, p1] 3(2:3:2:3) times.
Next row: [K1, p1] 3(2:3:2:3) times, k3, [p1, k5] to
last 4 sts, p1, k3.
Next row: K1, p2, [k1, p5] to last 10(8:10:8:10) sts,
k1, p2, k1, [k1, p1] 3(2:3:2:3) times.
Next row: [K1, p1] 3(2:3:2:3) times, k1, [k2tog,
yo, k1, yo, ssk, p1] to last 6 sts, k2tog, yo, k1, yo,
ssk, k1.
Next row: K1, [p5, k1] to last 6(4:6:4:6) sts,
[k1, p1] 3(2:3:2:3) times.
Rep last 8 rows once more.
Maintaining centre rib, work 5 rows st st.
Shape armhole
Next row (WS): Cast off 1 st, p to end of row
maintaining centre rib. 24(28:30:34:36) sts
Cont in st st maintaining centre rib, dec 1 st at
armhole edge of next and every alt row for 6 rows.
21(25:27:31:33) sts
Work 2 more rows st st without shaping for sizes
12–18 and 18–24 only.
Leave sts on a stitch holder.

Using 3mm needles, cast on 25(25:31:31:31) sts.
Row 1 (RS): [K1, p1] to last st, k1.
Row 2: [P1, k1] to last st, p1.
Rep rows 1–2 once more.
Change to 3.5mm needles.
Starting with a k row, work in st st and inc 1 st at
each end of every 4th(4th:8th:9th:12th) row for
12(12:24:28:36) rows. 31(31:37:37:37) sts
Next row: K6, [p1, k5] to last st, k1.
Next row: K1, [p5, k1] to end of row.
Next row: K1, [yo, ssk, p1, k2tog, yo, k1] to end
of row.
Next row: K1, p2, [k1, p5] to last 4 sts, k1, p2, k1.
Next row: K3, [p1, k5] to last 4 sts, p1, k3.
Next row: K1, p2, [k1, p5] to last 4 sts, k1, p2, k1.
Next row: K1, [k2tog, yo, k1, yo, ssk, p1] to last
6 sts, k2tog, yo, k1, yo, ssk, k1.
Next row: K1, [p5, k1] to end of row.
Rep last 8 rows once more.
Work 4 rows st st.
Shape sleeve top
Next row (RS): Cast off 1 st, k to end of row.
30(30:36:36:36) sts
Next row: Cast off 1 st, p to end of row.
29(29:35:35:35) sts
Cont in st st, dec 1 st at each end of next and
every alt row for 6 rows. 23(23:29:29:29) sts
Work 2 more rows st st without shaping for sizes

Lace Cardigan

12–18 and 18–24 only.
Leave sts on a stitch holder.

JOINING THE PIECES

RS facing, slip sts from stitch holders onto 3.5mm needle in this order: left front, sleeve, back, sleeve, right front. *121(137:159:173:181) sts*
You may find it easier to work on a long circular needle because of the number of sts, but continue to work in rows not in the round.
Work a dec row across all sts together as folls:
SIZE 3–6 ONLY
Row 1: [K1, p1] 3 times, k6, p1, k2, k3tog, k2, p1 across right front (*19 sts*); k2, k3tog, k2, p1, k5, p1, k2, k3tog, k2, p2tog across sleeve (*18 sts*); [k2, k3tog, k2, p1] 3 times, k2, k3tog, k2, p2tog across back (*24 sts*); k2, k3tog, k2, p1, k5, p1, k2, k3tog, k2, p2tog across sleeve (*18 sts*); k2, k4tog, k2, p1, k6, [p1, k1] 3 times across left front (*18 sts*).
SIZE 6–9 ONLY
Row 1: [K1, p1] twice, k6, p1, k2, k3tog, k2, p1, k5, p1 across right front (*23 sts*); k2, k3tog, k2, p1, k5, p1, k2, k3tog, k2, p2tog across sleeve (*18 sts*); [k2, k3tog, k2, p1] 4 times, k2, k3tog, k2, p2tog across back (*30 sts*); k2, k3tog, k2, p1, k5, p1, k2, k3tog, k2, p2tog across sleeve (*18 sts*); k5, p1, k2, k4tog, k2, p1, k6, [p1, k1] twice across left front (*22 sts*).

SIZE 9–12 ONLY
Row 1: [K1, p1] 3 times, k6, p1, k2, k3tog, k2, p1, k5, p1 across right front (*25 sts*); [k1, (k3tog) twice, k2, p1] twice, k2, k3tog, k2, p2tog across sleeve (*18 sts*); [k2, k3tog, k2, p1] 5 times, k2, k2tog, k2, p1 across back (*36 sts*); [k1, (k3tog) twice, k2, p1] twice, k2, k3tog, k2, p2tog across sleeve (*18 sts*); k5, p1, k2, k4tog, k2, p1, k6, [p1, k1] 3 times across left front (*24 sts*).
SIZE 12–18 ONLY
Row 1: [K1, p1] twice, k6, p1, [k2, k2tog, k2, p1] twice, k5, p1 across right front (*29 sts*); k2, k3tog, k2, [p1, k5] twice, p1, k2, k3tog, k2, p2tog across sleeve (*24 sts*); [k2, k4tog, k2, p1] 5 times, k2, k3tog, k2, p1 across back (*36 sts*); k2, k3tog, k2, [p1, k5] twice, p1, k2, k3tog, k2, p2tog across sleeve (*24 sts*); k5, p1, k2, k3tog, k2, p1, k2, k2tog, k2, p1, k6, [p1, k1] twice across left front (*28 sts*).
SIZE 18–24 ONLY
Row 1: [K1, p1] 3 times, k6, p1, [k2, k2tog, k2, p1] twice, k5, p1 across right front (*31 sts*); k2, k3tog, k2, [p1, k5] twice, p1, k2, k3tog, k2, p2tog across sleeve (*24 sts*); [k2, k3tog, k2, p1] 5 times, k2, k2tog, k2, p1, k2, k4tog, k2, p2tog across back (*42 sts*); k2, k3tog, k2, [p1, k5] twice, p1, k2, k3tog, k2, p2tog across sleeve (*24 sts*); k5, p1, k2, k3tog, k2, p1, k2, k2tog, k2, p1, k6, [p1, k1] 3 times across left front (*30 sts*).
97(111:121:141:151) sts in total

ALL SIZES

Row 2 (WS): [P1, k1] 3(2:3:2:3) times, k1, [p5, k1] to last 6(4:6:4:6) sts, [k1, p1] 3(2:3:2:3) times.

Row 3: [K1, p1] 3(2:3:2:3) times, k1, [yo, ssk, p1, k2tog, yo, k1] to last 6(4:6:4:6) sts, [p1, k1] 3(2:3:2:3) times.

Row 4: [P1, k1] 3(2:3:2:3) times, k1, p2, [k1, p5] to last 10(8:10:8:10:8) sts, k1, p2, k1, [k1, p1] 3(2:3:2:3) times.

Row 5: [K1, p1] 3(2:3:2:3) times, k3, [p1, k5] to last 10(8:10:8:10) sts, p1, k3, [p1, k1] 3(2:3:2:3) times.

Row 6: As row 4.

Row 7: [K1, p1] 3(2:3:2:3) times, k1, [k2tog, yo, k1, yo, ssk, p1] to last 12(10:12:12:10) sts, k2tog, yo, k1, yo, ssk, k1, [p1, k1] 3(2:3:2:3) times.

Row 8: As row 2.

Row 9: [K1, p1] 3(2:3:2:3) times, k6, [p1, k5] to last 7(5:7:5:7) sts, k1, [p1, k1] 3(2:3:2:3) times.

Rep rows 2–8 once more.

Work another dec row as folls:

Next row: [K1, p1] 3(2:3:2:3) times, k5, sk2po, [k3, sk2po] 12(15:16:20:21) times, k5, [p1, k1] 3(2:3:2:3) times. *71(79:87:99:107) sts*

Next row: Purl, maintaining rib at centre front edges.

SIZE 3–6 ONLY

Next row: [K1, p1] 3 times, k3, k2tog, k1, [k2tog, k6] 6 times, k2tog, k3, [p1, k1] 3 times. *63 sts*

SIZE 6–9 ONLY

Next row: [K1, p1] twice, k4, [sk2po, k5] 4 times, k4, [sk2po, k5] 3 times, sk2po, k4, [p1, k1] twice. *63 sts*

SIZE 9–12 ONLY

Work 2 rows as set.

Next row: [K1, p1] 3 times, k3, [ssk, k2] 17 times, k2tog, k2, [p1, k1] 3 times. *69 sts*

SIZE 12–18 ONLY

Work 2 rows as set.

Next row: [K1, p1] twice, k5, [ssk, k1, k2tog] 16 times, k6, [p1, k1] twice. *67 sts*

SIZE 18–24 ONLY

Next row: [K1, p1] 3 times, k6, [ssk, k1] 28 times, k5, [p1, k1] 3 times. *79 sts*

ALL SIZES

Next row: Purl, maintaining rib at centre front edges.

Work 2 rows st st, maintaining rib at centre front edges.

Next row: [K1, p1] to last st, k1.

Next row: [P1, k1] to last st, p1.

Next row: [K1, p1] to last st, k1.

Cast off.

TO MAKE UP

Weave in loose ends.
Press the pieces following directions on the ball band.
Sew up the armhole seams. Sew up the underarm and side seams from end of sleeve to lower edge of body.
Sew on 4 or 5 buttons along left front rib. You do not need to make buttonholes because the buttons used are quite small; simply push the buttons through the right front rib to close.

Lace Cardigan

Wide Collar Jacket

This jacket is good for covering up on colder days but can also be used as a cardigan.

MEASUREMENTS

Size	0–3 mths	3–6 mths	6–9 mths	9–12 mths	12–18 mths	18–24 mths
Finished chest measurement	46cm	51cm	56cm	61cm	63cm	66cm
Finished sleeve seam	10.5cm	10.5cm	14cm	14cm	17cm	17cm

YARN

3(3:3:4:4:5) x 50g balls of Debbie Bliss Rialto Aran in Denim 21203

MATERIALS

Pair each of 3.5mm and 4.5mm knitting needles
5 stitch holders
Tapestry needle
3.5mm crochet hook
3 x 12mm buttons
Sewing needle and thread
Small piece of fabric for front panel, approx 15 cm x 30cm

TENSION

16 sts and 23 rows over st st using 4.5mm needles

ABBREVIATIONS

See page 140

BACK

Using 3.5mm needles, cast on
37(41:45:49:51:53) sts.
Row 1 (RS): [K1, p1] to last st, k1.
Row 2: [P1, k1] to last st, p1.
Change to 4.5mm needles.
Row 3: K1(3:1:3:4:1), [yo, k2(2:3:3:3:4), ssk,
k2tog, k2(2:3:3:3:4), yo, k1] 4 times, k0(2:0:2:3:0).
Row 4: Purl.
Rep rows 3–4, 3 times more.
Starting with a k row, cont in st st until back
measures 12(13:15:17:19:21)cm from cast-on
edge, ending with a p row.
Shape raglan armholes
Cast off 2 sts at each end of next 2 rows.
33(37:41:45:47:49) sts
Dec 1 st at each end of next and every alt row
until there are 11(15:19:19:19:21) sts.
Leave sts on a stitch holder.

LEFT FRONT

Using 3.5mm needles, cast on
19(21:23:25:27:29) sts.
Row 1 (RS): [K1, p1] to last st, k1.
Row 2: [P1, k1] to last st, p1.
Change to 4.5mm needles.
Row 3: K1(2:1:2:3:2), [yo, k2(2:3:3:3:4), ssk,
k2tog, k2(2:3:3:3:4), yo, k1] twice, k0(1:0:1:2:1).

Row 4: Purl.
Rep rows 3–4, 3 times more.
Starting with a k row, work in st st until left front
measures 12(13:15:17:19:21)cm from cast-on
edge, ending with a p row.
Shape raglan armhole
Next row: Cast off 2 sts, k to end of row.
17(19:21:23:25:27) sts
Next row: Purl.
Cont in st st, dec 1 st at beg of next and every alt
row until there are 6(8:9:10:11:13) sts.
Leave sts on a stitch holder.

RIGHT FRONT

Using 3.5mm needles, cast on
19(21:23:25:27:29) sts.
Row 1 (RS): [K1, p1] to last st, k1.
Row 2: [P1, k1] to last st, p1.
Change to 4.5mm needles.
Row 3: K1(2:1:2:3:2), [yo, k2(2:3:3:3:4), ssk,
k2tog, k2(2:3:3:3:4), yo, k1] twice, k0(1:0:1:2:1).
Row 4: Purl.
Rep rows 3–4, 3 times more.
Starting with a k row, work in st st until right front
measures 12(13:15:17:19:21)cm from cast-on
edge, ending with a p row.
Shape raglan armhole
Next row: Knit.
Next row: Cast off 2 sts, p to end of row.

Wide Collar Jacket

17(19:21:23:25:27) sts
Cont in st st, dec 1 st at end of next and every alt row until there are 6(8:9:10:11:13) sts.
Leave sts on a stitch holder.

SLEEVE (MAKE TWO)

Using 3.5mm needles, cast on
22(24:26:26:26:28) sts.
Row 1 (RS): [K1, p1].
Row 2: As row 1.
Change to 4.5mm needles.
Starting with a knit (RS) row, cont in st st, inc 1 st at each end of every 8th row until there are 28(30:34:34:36:38) sts.
Shape raglan sleeve top
Cast off 2 sts at beg of next 2 rows.
24(26:30:30:32:34) sts
Dec 1 st at each end of next and every foll 4th row until there are 18(20:22:20:20:22) sts, then at each end of every alt row until there are 6(8:12:12:14:16) sts.
Leave sts on a stitch holder.

COLLAR

RS facing, slip sts from stitch holders onto 3.5mm needle in this order: left front, sleeve, back, sleeve, right front. *35(47:61:63:69:79) sts*

SIZE 0–3 ONLY
Row 1: [K4, m1] 8 times, k3. *43 sts*
Work row 2.
ALL OTHER SIZES
Row 1 (RS): [K1, p1] to last st, k1.
Row 2: [P1, k1] to last st, p1.
Cont in rib as set until collar measures
8(9:10:11:12:13)cm.
Cast off.

FRONT PANEL

Using 3.5mm needles, cast on
28(32:34:38:40:42) sts.
Row 1 (RS): [K1, p1].
Row 2: As row 1.
Row 3: K1(3:1:3:4:2), [yo, k2(2:3:3:3:4), ssk,
k2tog, k2(2:3:3:3:4), yo, k1] 3 times, k0(2:0:2:3:1).
Row 4: Purl.
Rep rows 3–4, 3 times more.
Next row: Knit.
Cast off.

TO MAKE UP

Weave in loose ends.
Press the pieces following directions on the
ball band.
Sew up the raglans. Sew up the underarm and
side seams from end of sleeve to lower edge
of body.
Sew cast-off edge of front panel to left front of
jacket. Work a simple crochet edging (such as
double crochet) around the outer edge of the
panel, making a small chain loop at each pointed
tip for buttonholes (3 in total). Fold the front
panel over the right front of the jacket and sew
on buttons to match.
Fold a piece of fabric in half so that it is double-
sided and cut out a piece to match the knitted
front panel. Using chain stitch, machine or
hand-sew the fabric panel to the right front of
the jacket.

Wide Collar Jacket

Small Cable Cardigan

This cardigan is made in the same cable design as the Small Cable Sweater, but with five buttons down one side.

MEASUREMENTS

Size	0–3 mths	3–6 mths	6–12 mths	12–18 mths	18–24 mths
Finished chest measurement	47cm	50cm	58cm	61cm	68cm
Finished sleeve seam	12cm	12cm	17cm	18cm	21cm

YARN

2(2:3:3:4) x 50g balls of Debbie Bliss Baby Cashmerino in Dusty Rose 340608

MATERIALS

Pair each of 3mm and 4mm knitting needles
Long 4mm circular needle
Cable needle
4 stitch holders
Tapestry needle
5 x 12mm buttons
Sewing needle and thread

TENSION

30 sts and 28 rows to 10cm over reverse st st using 4mm needles
9-st cable panel (C4B, k1, C4F) measures 4.5cm wide

C2B – slip next 1 st onto cable needle and hold at back of work, knit next 1 st from left-hand needle, then knit 1 st from cable needle.

C2F – slip next 1 st onto cable needle and hold at front of work, knit next 1 st from left-hand needle, then knit 1 st from cable needle.

C3B – slip next 2 sts onto cable needle and hold at back of work, knit next 1 st from left-hand needle, then knit 2 sts from cable needle.

C3F – slip next 1 st onto cable needle and hold at front of work, knit next 2 sts from left-hand needle, then knit 1 st from cable needle.

C4B – slip next 3 sts onto cable needle and hold at back of work, knit next 1 st from left-hand needle, then knit 3 sts from cable needle.

C4F – slip next 1 st onto cable needle and hold at front of work, knit next 3 sts from left-hand needle, then knit 1 st from cable needle.

See also page 140

BACK

Using 3mm needles, cast on 53(57:65:69:75) sts.
Row 1: [P1, k1] to last st, p1.
Row 2: [K1, p1] to last st, k1.
Row 3: As row 1.
Change to 4mm needles.

Row 4 (RS): P4(6:4:6:3), [k9, p3] 3(3:4:4:5) times, k9, p4(6:4:6:3).
Row 5: Knit the purl sts and purl the knit sts of previous row.
Row 6: P4(6:4:6:3), [C4B, k1, C4F, p3] 3(3:4:4:5) times, C4B, k1, C4F, p4(6:4:6:3).
Row 7: As row 5.
Rep rows 4–7, 7(8:9:10:11) times more.
Leave sts on a stitch holder.

FRONT

Using 3mm needles, cast on 51(54:63:66:73) sts.
Row 1: [P1, k1] to last 1(0:1:0:1) sts, p1(0:1:0:1).
Row 2: K1(0:1:0:1), [p1, k1] to end of row.
Row 3: As row 1.
Change to 4mm needles.
Row 4 (RS): P4(6:4:6:3), [k9, p3] 3(3:4:4:5) times, k9, p2(3:2:3:1).
Row 5: Knit the purl sts and purl the knit sts of previous row.
Row 6: P4(6:4:6:3), [C4B, k1, C4F, p3] 3(3:4:4:5) times, C4B, k1, C4F, p2(3:2:3:1).
Row 7: As row 5.
Rep rows 4–7, 7(8:9:10:11) times more.
Leave sts on a stitch holder.

Small Cable Cardigan

Sleeve (make two)

Using 3mm needles, cast on 27(29:33:33:35) sts.
Row 1: [P1, k1] to last st, p1.
Row 2: [K1, p1] to last st, k1.
Row 3: As row 1.
Change to 4mm needles.
Row 4 (RS): P3(4:0:0:1), k9, p3, k9, p3(4:3:3:3), k0(0:9:9:9), p0(0:0:0:1).
Row 5: Knit the purl sts and purl the knit sts of previous row.
Row 6 (cable row): P3(4:0:0:1), C4B, k1, C4F, p3, C4B, k1, C4F, p3(4:3:3:3), [C4B, k1, C4F] 0(0:1:1:1) times, p0(0:0:0:1).
Row 7: As row 5.
Cont in cable patt as set by rows 4–7, and at the same time inc and work as purl 1 st at each end of next cable row and then every alt cable row until there are 35(37:41:45:49) sts, ending with a patt row 7.
SIZE 6–12 ONLY
Work another 12 rows ending with a patt row.
Leave sts on a stitch holder.

Joining the pieces

RS facing, slip sts from stitch holders onto 4mm circular needle in this order: front, sleeve, back, sleeve. *174(185:210:225:246) sts*

It is easier to use a long circular needle because of the number of sts, but continue to work in rows not in the round.
Cont in cable patt as set by rows 4–7 above, starting with a patt row 4 and shaping as folls:
Row 1 (RS): Work in patt and purl edge sts as set.
Row 2 and all WS rows: Knit the purl sts and purl the knit sts of previous row.
Row 3 (CR – cable row): Patt to end of row, working a double dec (p3tog) at each raglan armhole between the sleeves and body pieces but not at each end of row. *168(179:204:219:240) sts*
Row 5: P5(6:2:4:6), p2tog, then work patt and double dec at each raglan armhole as before but not at end of row. *161(172:197:212:233) sts*
Row 7 (CR): As row 3, but work a single dec (p2tog) instead of a double dec at armholes for size 6–12 only. *155(166:194:206:227) sts*
Row 9: P4(5:1:3:5), p2tog, patt to end of row. *154(165:193:205:226) sts*
Row 11 (CR): As row 3, but do not dec at armholes for size 6–12 only. *148(159:193:199:220) sts*
Row 13: Patt to end of row, dec 3 sts at armholes for size 3–6 only and dec 1 st at armholes for size 12–18 only. *148(150:193:196:220) sts*
There should now be 3 sts between cable panels plus edge sts at each end of row.
Row 15 (CR): Patt to end of row, working a single dec (p2tog) between cable panels but not at each end of row. *137(139:178:181:203) sts*

Row 17: Patt to end of row.
Row 19 (CR): Patt to end of row.
Row 21: P5(6:2:4:6), [k3, sk2po, k3, p2] to last 11(12:11:12:10) sts, k3, sk2po, k3, p2(3:2:3:1). *113(115:146:149:167) sts*
Row 23 (CR): P5(6:2:4:6), [C3B, k1, C3F, p2] to last 9(10:9:10:8) sts, C3B, k1, C3F, p2(3:2:3:1).
Row 25: Patt to end of row, working a single dec (p2tog) between cable panels **but not** at each end of row. *102(104:131:134:150) sts*
Row 27 (CR): Patt to end of row.
SIZES 0–3, 3–6 AND 6–12 ONLY
Row 29: P5(6:2), [k2, sk2po, k2, p1] to last 9(10:9) sts, k2, sk2po, k2, p2(3:2). *78(80:99) sts*
Row 31 (CR): P5(6:2), [C2B, k1, C2F, p1] to last 7(8:7) sts, C2B, k1, C2F, p2(3:2).
Row 33: P5(6:2), [k1, sk2po, k1, p1] to last 7(8:7) sts, k1, sk2po, k1, p2(3:2). *54(56:67) sts*
Change to 3mm needles.
Row 35: [K1, p1] to end of row, and **at the same time** dec 1 st in centre for size 6–12 only. *54(56:66) sts*
Row 36: [K1, p1] to end of row.
Cast off.
SIZES 12–18 AND 18–24 ONLY
Row 29: Patt to end of row.
Row 31 (CR): Patt to end of row.
Row 33: P4(6), [k2, sk2po, k2, p1] to last 10(8) sts, k2, sk2po, k2, p3(1). *102(114) sts*
Row 35 (CR): P4(6), [C2B, k1, C2F, p1] to last 8(6) sts, C2B, k1, C2F, p3(1).
Row 37: Patt to end of row.

Row 39 (CR): Patt to end of row.
Row 41: P4(6), [k1, sk2po, k1, p1] to last 8(6) sts, k1, sk2po, k1, p3(1). *70(78) sts*
Row 42: As row 2.
Change to 3mm needles.
Row 43: [K1, p1] to end of row.
Row 44: As row 43.
Cast off.

TO MAKE UP

Weave in loose ends.
Press the piece following directions on the ball band.
Sew up the left raglan seams. Sew up the left underarm and side seam from end of sleeve to lower edge of body.
Sew up the back seam of the right raglan.
Sew up the right underarm seam from end of sleeve to armhole.
Using 3mm needles and with RS facing, pick up 53(57:61:71:75) sts along open edge of front. Work k1, p1 rib for 2(2:4:4:4) rows, then cast off. Repeat along open edge of back, from lower edge of body to top of front right sleeve raglan.
Sew on 5 buttons evenly spaced along the rib edging on the back and sleeve. You do not need to make buttonholes because the buttons used are quite small; simply push the buttons through the rib edging on the front to close.

Small Cable Cardigan

Garter Stitch Cardigan

Garter stitch with a small wave in the middle – simple but effective. A crochet edge can be worked along the centre for buttonholes.

MEASUREMENTS

Size	0–3 mths	3–6 mths	6–12 mths	12–18 mths	18–24 mths
Finished chest measurement	47cm	52cm	56cm	61cm	65cm
Finished sleeve seam	11.5cm	14.5cm	17cm	20cm	22.5cm

YARN

2(2:3:3:4) x 50g balls of Rowan Cashsoft DK in Blue Jacket 535

MATERIALS

Pair of 4mm knitting needles
5 stitch holders
Tapestry needle
4mm crochet hook
5 x 12mm buttons
Sewing needle and thread

TENSION

18 sts and 36 rows to 10cm over garter stitch patt using 4mm needles

ABBREVIATIONS

See page 140

Note: Stitches are made and lost in the stitch pattern. These made and lost stitches are not included in any stitch counts beyond row 12.

Back

Cast on 42(46:50:54:58) sts.
Rows 1–2: Knit.
Row 3 (RS): K13(15:17:19:21), yo, k16, yo, k13(15:17:19:21). *44(48:52:56:60) sts*
Row 4 and all WS rows: Knit.
Row 5: K14(16:18:20:22), yo, k16, yo, k14(16:18:20:22). *46(50:54:58:62) sts*
Row 7: K15(17:19:21:23), yo, k16, yo, k15(17:19:21:23). *48(52:56:60:64) sts*
Row 9: K16(18:20:22:24), yo, k16, yo, k16(18:20:22:24). *50(54:58:62:66) sts*
Row 11: K17(19:21:23:25), [k2tog] 8 times, k17(19:21:23:25). *42(46:50:54:58) sts*
Row 12: Knit.
Rep rows 3–12, 3(3:4:5:5) times more.
Shape raglan armholes
Cont in patt as set, casting off 1 st at beg of next 2 rows. *40(44:48:52:56) sts*
Dec 1 st at each end of next and every foll 3rd row for 18(26:38:38:48) rows. *28(26:22:26:24) sts*
Leave sts on a stitch holder.

Left front

Cast on 22(24:26:28:30) sts.
Rows 1–2: Knit.
Row 3 (RS): K13(15:17:19:21), yo, k9. *23(25:27:29:31) sts*
Row 4 and all WS rows: Knit.
Row 5: K14(16:18:20:22), yo, k9. *24(26:28:30:32) sts*
Row 7: K15(17:19:21:23), yo, k9. *25(27:29:31:33) sts*
Row 9: K16(18:20:22:24), yo, k9. *26(28:30:32:34) sts*
Row 11: K17(19:21:23:25), [k2tog] 4 times, k1. *22(24:26:28:30) sts*
Row 12: Knit.
Rep rows 3–12, 3(3:4:5:5) times more.
Shape raglan armhole
Next row: Cast off 1 st, patt to end of row. 21(23:25:27:29) sts
Next row: Knit.
Cont in patt as set, dec 1 st at armhole edge of next and every foll 3rd row for 18(26:38:38:48) rows. *15(14:12:14:13) sts*
Leave sts on a stitch holder.

Garter Stitch Cardigan

RIGHT FRONT

Cast on 22(24:26:28:30) sts.
Rows 1–2: Knit.
Row 3 (RS): K9, yo, k13(15:17:19:21).
23(25:27:29:31) sts
Row 4 and all WS rows: Knit.
Row 5: K9, yo, k14(16:18:20:22).
24(26:28:30:32) sts
Row 7: K9, yo, k15(17:19:21:23).
25(27:29:31:33) sts
Row 9: K9, yo, k16(18:20:22:24).
26(28:30:32:34) sts
Row 11: K1, [k2tog] 4 times, k17(19:21:23:25).
22(24:26:28:30) sts
Row 12: Knit.
Rep rows 3–12, 3(3:4:5:5) times more.
Shape raglan armhole
Next row: Patt to end of row.
Next row: Cast off 1 st, k to end of row.
21(23:25:27:29) sts
Cont in patt as set, dec 1 st at armhole edge of
next and every foll 3rd row for 18(26:38:38:48)
rows. *15(14:12:14:13) sts*
Leave sts on a stitch holder.

SLEEVE (MAKE TWO)

Cast on 22(24:26:28:30) sts.
Rows 1–2: Knit.
Row 3 (RS): K3(4:5:6:7), yo, k16, yo, k3(4:5:6:7).
24(26:28:30:32) sts
Row 4 and all WS rows: Knit.
Row 5: K4(5:6:7:8), yo, k16, yo, k4(5:6:7:8).
26(28:30:32:34) sts
Row 7: K5(6:7:8:9), yo, k16, yo, k5(6:7:8:9).
28(30:32:34:36) sts
Row 9: K6(7:8:9:10), yo, k16, yo, k6(7:8:9:10).
30(32:34:36:38) sts
Row 11: K7(8:9:10:11), [k2tog] 8 times,
k7(8:9:10:11). *22(24:26:28:30) sts*
Row 12: Knit.
Cont in patt as set, inc 1 st at each end of next and
every foll 7th(8th:12th:12th:14th) row until there
are 30(34:34:38:40) sts.
Patt 8(7:13:16:13) rows without shaping.
Shape raglan armholes
Keeping patt correct as set, cast off 1 st at beg of
next 2 rows. *28(32:32:36:38) sts*
Dec 1 st at each end at next and every foll 3rd row
for 15(17:18:21:27) rows. *18(20:20:22:20) sts*
Cont in patt while there are sufficient sts, then
work in garter stitch after final patt repeat has been
worked, and at the same time dec 1 st at each end
of next and every foll 2nd(2nd:3rd:2nd:3rd) row
for 3(9:20:17:21) rows. *14(10:6:4:6) sts*
Leave sts on a stitch holder.

RS facing, slip sts from stitch holders onto needle in this order: left front, sleeve, back, sleeve, right front. *86(74:58:62:62) sts*

SIZE 0–3 ONLY

Next row (RS): K12, k2tog, k2, ssk, k8, k2tog, k2, ssk, k22, k2tog, k2, ssk, k8, k2tog, k2, ssk, k12. *78 sts*

Next row: Knit.

Next row: K11, k2tog, k2, ssk, k6, k2tog, k2, ssk, k20, k2tog, k2, ssk, k6, k2tog, k2, ssk, k11. *70 sts*

Next row: Knit.

Next row: K10, k2tog, k2, ssk, k4, k2tog, k2, ssk, k18, k2tog, k2, ssk, k4, k2tog, k2, ssk, k10. *62 sts*

Next row: Knit.

Next row: K9, k2tog, k2, ssk, k2, k2tog, k2, ssk, k16, k2tog, k2, ssk, k2, k2tog, k2, ssk, k9. *54 sts*

Cast off.

SIZE 3–6 ONLY

Next row (RS): K11, k2tog, k2, ssk, k4, k2tog, k2, ssk, k20, k2tog, k2, ssk, k4, k2tog, k2, ssk, k11. *66 sts*

Next row: K10, k2tog, k2, ssk, k2, k2tog, k2, ssk, k18, k2tog, k2, ssk, k2, k2tog, k2, ssk, k10. *58 sts*

Cast off.

ALL REMAINING SIZES

Knit 5 rows.

Cast off.

Weave in loose ends.

Steam the piece following directions on the ball band.

Sew up the raglans. Sew up the underarm and side seams from end of sleeve to lower edge of body.

Work a simple crochet edging (such as double crochet) with 5 small evenly spaced chain loops for buttonholes along the right front edge.

Crochet a similar edging without loops along the left front edge. Sew buttons onto the left front edge to match the buttonholes.

Garter Stitch Cardigan

Garter Stitch Jacket

This is worked in thicker yarn than the Garter Stitch Cardigan, to use as a jacket when the weather gets cold.

MEASUREMENTS

Size	0–3 mths	3–6 mths	6–12 mths	12–18 mths	18–24 mths
Finished chest measurement	44cm	49cm	56cm	62cm	66cm
Finished sleeve seam	9cm	9cm	12cm	15cm	15cm

YARN

1(2:2:2:3) x 100g skein of Malabrigo Merino Worsted in Dusty 60

MATERIALS

Pair of 5mm knitting needles
5 stitch holders
Tapestry needle
5mm crochet hook
3 x 12mm buttons
Sewing needle and thread

TENSION

16 sts and 34 rows to 10cm over garter stitch patt using 5mm needles

ABBREVIATIONS

See page 140

Note: Stitches are made and lost in the stitch pattern. These made and lost stitches are not included in any stitch counts beyond row 12.

BACK

Cast on 34(38:44:48:52) sts.
Rows 1–2: Knit.
Row 3 (RS): K9(11:14:16:18), yo, k16, yo, k9(11:14:16:18). *36(40:46:50:54) sts*
Row 4 and all WS rows: Knit.
Row 5: K10(12:15:17:19), yo, k16, yo, k10(12:15:17:19). *38(42:48:52:56) sts*
Row 7: K11(13:16:18:20), yo, k16, yo, k11(13:16:18:20). *40(44:50:54:58) sts*
Row 9: K12(14:17:19:21), yo, k16, yo, k12(14:17:19:21). *42(46:52:56:60) sts*
Row 11: K13(15:18:20:22), [k2tog] 8 times, k13(15:18:20:22). *34(38:44:48:52) sts*
Row 12: Knit.
Rep rows 3–12, 3(3:4:5:5) times more.
Shape raglan armholes
Cont in patt as set, casting off 1 st at beg of next 2 rows. *32(36:42:46:50) sts*
Dec 1 st at each end of every 3rd row for 18(28:28:38:38) rows. *20(18:24:22:26) sts*
Leave sts on a stitch holder.

Left front

Cast on 18(20:23:25:27) sts.

Rows 1–2: Knit.

Row 3 (RS): K9(11:14:16:18), yo, k9.
19(21:24:26:28) sts

Row 4 and all WS rows: Knit.

Row 5: K10(12:15:17:19), yo, k9.
20(22:25:27:29) sts

Row 7: K11(13:16:18:20), yo, k9.
21(23:26:28:30) sts

Row 9: K12(14:17:19:21), yo, k9
22(24:27:29:31) sts

Row 11: K13(15:18:20:22), [k2tog] 4 times, k1.
18(20:23:25:27) sts

Row 12: Knit.

Rep rows 3–12, 3(3:4:5:5) times more.

Shape raglan armhole

Next row: Cast off 1 st, patt to end of row.
17(19:22:24:26) sts

Next row: Patt to end of row.

Cont in patt as set, dec 1 st at armhole edge of every 3rd row for 18(28:28:38:38) rows.
11(10:13:12:14) sts

Leave sts on a stitch holder.

Right front

Cast on 18(20:23:25:27) sts.

Rows 1–2: Knit.

Row 3 (RS): K9, yo, k9(11:14:16:18).
19(21:24:26:28) sts

Row 4 and all WS rows: Knit.

Row 5: K9, yo, k10(12:15:17:19).
20(22:25:27:29) sts

Row 7: K9, yo, k11(13:16:18:20).
21(23:26:28:30) sts

Row 9: K9, yo, k12(14:17:19:21).
22(24:27:29:31) sts

Row 11: K1, [k2tog] 4 times, k13(15:18:20:22).
18(20:23:25:27) sts

Row 12: Knit.

Rep rows 3–12, 3(3:4:5:5) times more.

Shape raglan armhole

Next row: Patt to end of row.

Next row: Cast off 1 st, patt to end of row.
17(19:22:24:26) sts

Cont in patt as set, dec 1 st at armhole edge of every 3rd row for 18(28:28:38:38) rows.
11(10:13:12:14) sts

Leave sts on a stitch holder.

Garter Stitch Jacket

SLEEVE (MAKE TWO)

Cast on 26(28:30:32:34) sts.
Rows 1–2: Knit.
Row 3 (RS): K5(6:7:8:9), yo, k16, yo, k5(6:7:8:9).
28(30:32:34:36) sts
Row 4 and all WS rows: Knit.
Row 5: K6(7:8:9:10), yo, k16, yo, k6(7:8:9:10).
30(32:34:36:38) sts
Row 7: K7(8:9:10:11), yo, k16, yo, k7(8:9:10:11).
32(34:36:38:40) sts
Row 9: K8(9:10:11:12), yo, k16, yo,
k8(9:10:11:12). *34(36:38:40:42) sts*
Row 11: K9(10:11:12:13), [k2tog] 8 times,
k9(10:11:12:13). *26(28:30:32:34) sts*
Row 12: Knit.
Rep rows 3–12, 2(2:3:4:4) times more.

Shape raglan sleeve top
Keeping patt correct as set, cast off 1 st at each
end of next 2 rows. *24(26:28:30:32) sts*
Cont in patt while there are sufficient sts, then
work in garter stitch after final patt repeat has
been worked, and at the same time dec 1 st at
each end of every 3rd row for 8(28:28:28:28)
rows. *20(8:10:12:14) sts*
SIZE 0–3 ONLY
Work 10 rows garter stitch, dec 1 st at each end of
next and every alt row. *10 sts*
SIZES 12–18 AND 18–24 ONLY

Work 10 rows garter stitch, dec 1 st at each end of
next and every foll 3rd row. *4(6) sts*
ALL SIZES
Leave sts on a stitch holder.

JOINING THE PIECES

RS facing, slip sts from stitch holders onto needle
in this order: left front, sleeve, back, sleeve, right
front. *62(54:70:54:66) sts*
SIZE 0–3 ONLY
Next row (RS): K8, k2tog, k2, ssk, k4, k2tog, k2,
ssk, k14, k2tog, k2, ssk, k4, k2tog, k2, ssk, k8.
54 sts
Next row: Knit.
Next row: K7, k2tog, k10, ssk, k12, k2tog, k10,
ssk, k7. *50 sts*
SIZE 3–6 ONLY
Next row (RS): K7, k2tog, k2, ssk, k2, k2tog, k2,
ssk, k12, k2tog, k2, ssk, k2, k2tog, k2, ssk, k7.
46 sts
SIZE 6–12 ONLY
Next row (RS): K9, k2tog, k2, ssk, k8, k2tog, k2,
ssk, k12, k2tog, k2, ssk, k8, k2tog, k2, ssk, k9.
62 sts
Next row: Knit.
Next row: K8, k2tog, k14, ssk, k10, k2tog, k14,
ssk, k8. *58 sts*

Garter Stitch Jacket

SIZE 12–18 ONLY
Next row (RS): K9, k2tog, k6, ssk, k16, k2tog, k6, ssk, k9. *50 sts*
SIZE 18–24 ONLY
Next row (RS): K11, k2tog, k8, ssk, k20, k2tog, k8, ssk, k11. *62 sts*
Next row: Knit.
Next row: K10, k2tog, k8, ssk, k18, k2tog, k8, ssk, k10. *58 sts*
ALL SIZES
Knit 2 rows.
Cast off.

To make up

Weave in loose ends.
Steam the piece following directions on the ball band.
Sew up the raglans. Sew up the underarm and side seams from end of sleeve to lower edge of body.
Work a simple crochet edging (such as double crochet) along the right front edge, with 3 small chain loops for buttonholes evenly spaced along top half of edge. Crochet a similar edging without loops along the left front edge. Sew buttons onto the left front edge to match the buttonholes.

Hooded Jacket

If you can master a knit stitch and a purl stitch, this should
be something for you. It does require a bit of patience,
though, as it is a bit bigger than some of the other garments.
Knitted up in cotton, it can also be useful as a bathrobe.

MEASUREMENTS

Size	3–6 mths	6–9 mths	9–12 mths	12–18 mths	18–24 mths
Finished chest measurement	50cm	53cm	59cm	62cm	66cm
Finished sleeve seam	13.5cm	15cm	17cm	19cm	21cm

YARN

3(4:4:5:5) x 50g balls of MillaMia Naturally Soft Merino in Plum 162

MATERIALS

Pair of 3mm knitting needles
5 stitch holders
Tapestry needle

TENSION

22 sts and 31 rows to 10cm over patt using 3mm needles

ABBREVIATIONS

See page 140

BACK

Cast on 55(59:65:69:73) sts.

Row 1 (RS): [K1, p1] to last st, k1.

Row 2: [P1, k1] to last st, p1.

Rep rows 1–2 once more.

Row 5: [K1, p1] to last st, k1.

Row 6: Purl.

Row 7: [P1, k1] to last st, p1.

Row 8: [K1, p1] to last st, k1.

Rep rows 7–8 once more.

Row 11: [P1, k1] to last st, p1.

Row 12: Purl.

Rep rows 1–12, 2(3:3:4:4) times more.

Rep rows 1–6 once more for sizes 3–6, 9–12 and 18–24 only.

Shape raglan armholes

Keeping patt correct as set, cast off 2 sts at beg of next 2 rows. *51(55:61:65:69) sts*

Dec 1 st at each end of next and every alt row until there are 23(27:33:31:35) sts.

Leave sts on a stitch holder.

LEFT FRONT

Cast on 35(37:41:43:45) sts.
Row 1 (RS): [K1, p1] to last st, k1.
Row 2: [P1, k1] to last st, p1.
Rep rows 1–2 once more.
Row 5: [K1, p1] to last st, k1.
Row 6: Purl.
Row 7: [P1, k1] to last st, p1.
Row 8: [K1, p1] to last st, k1.
Rep rows 7–8 once more.
Row 11: [P1, k1] to last st, p1.
Row 12: Purl.
Rep rows 1–12, 2(3:3:4:4) times more.
Rep rows 1–6 once more for sizes 3–6, 9–12 and 18–24 only.

Shape raglan armhole
Next row: Cast off 2 sts, patt to end of row.
33(35:39:41:43) sts
Next row: Patt to end of row.
Keeping patt correct as set, dec 1 st at armhole edge of next and every alt row until there are 19(21:25:24:26) sts.
Leave sts on a stitch holder.

RIGHT FRONT

Cast on 35(37:41:43:45) sts.
Row 1 (RS): [K1, p1] to last st, k1.
Row 2: [P1, k1] to last st, p1.
Rep rows 1–2 once more.
Row 5: [K1, p1] to last st, k1.
Row 6: Purl.
Row 7: [P1, k1] to last st, p1.
Row 8: [K1, p1] to last st, k1.
Rep rows 7–8 once more.
Row 11: [P1, k1] to last st, p1.
Row 12: Purl.
Rep rows 1–12, 2(3:3:4:4) times more.
Rep rows 1–6 once more for sizes 3–6, 9–12 and 18–24 only.

Shape raglan armhole
Next row: Patt to end of row.
Next row: Cast off 2 sts, patt to end of row.
33(35:39:41:43) sts
Keeping patt correct as set, dec 1 st at armhole edge of next and every alt row until there are 19(21:25:24:26) sts.
Leave sts on a stitch holder.

Hooded Jacket

Sleeve (make two)

Cast on 27(29:31:33:35) sts.
Work in patt as set above, inc 1 st at each
end of every 6th (purl) row until there are
41(45:49:53:57) sts.
Shape raglan sleeve top
Cast off 2 sts at beg of next 2 rows.
37(41:45:49:53) sts
Dec 1 st at each end of next and every alt row
until there are 9(13:17:15:19) sts.
Leave sts on a stitch holder.

Hood

RS facing, slip sts from stitch holders onto needle
in this order: left front, sleeve, back, sleeve, right
front. *79(95:117:109:125) sts*
Next row (RS): Work across all sts in patt as set
and **at the same time** purl together the last and
first sts of each section where they join.
75(91:113:105:121) sts
Cont in patt until hood measures
20(22:23:25:26)cm.
Cast off.

To make up

Weave in loose ends.
Steam the pieces following directions on the
ball band.
Sew up the raglans. Sew up the underarm and
side seams from end of sleeve to lower edge of
body. Fold the hood in half and sew the top seam.

Hooded Jacket

Vests

3

Lace Vest

The lace pattern used for this vest is the same as for the Lace Cardigan. If you feel able to, you can choose to make the front and back a bit longer and this way make the vest into a little dress. Just remember to get extra yarn.

MEASUREMENTS

Size	3–6 mths	6–12 mths	12–18 mths	18–24 mths
Finished chest measurement	41cm	46cm	52cm	57cm

YARN

2 x 50g balls of Rowan Belle Organic DK by Amy Butler in Slate 015

MATERIALS

Pair of 3.5mm knitting needles
Stitch holder
Tapestry needle

TENSION

22 sts and 26 rows to 10cm over patt using 3.5mm needles

ABBREVIATIONS

See page 140

LACE PATTERN

(Worked over multiple of 6 sts + 1 st and 8 rows)
Row 1 (RS): K6, [p1, k5] to last st, k1.
Row 2: K1, [p5, k1] to end of row.
Row 3: K1, [yo, ssk, p1, k2tog, yo, k1] to end
of row.
Row 4: K1, p2, [k1, p5] to last 4 sts, k1, p2, k1.
Row 5: K3, [p1, k5] to last 4 sts, p1, k3.
Row 6: As row 4.
Row 7: K1, [k2tog, yo, k1, yo, ssk, p1] to end of
row but finish last repeat with k1 instead of p1.
Row 8: As row 2.

BACK

Cast on 45(51:57:63) sts.
Row 1 (RS): [K1, p1] to last st, k1.
Row 2: [P1, k1] to last st, p1.
Rep rows 1–2, 14(19:23:23) times more.
Shape armholes
Keeping rib patt correct as set, cast off 2 sts at beg
of next 2 rows. *41(47:53:59) sts*
Dec 1 st at each end of next and every alt row for
16 rows, working dec as folls: [k1, p1] 3 times, ssk,
[k1, p1] to last 8 sts, k2tog, [p1, k1] 3 times.
25(31:37:43) sts
Cont in rib for 6(10:10:10) rows.

Lace Vest

Shape neckline and straps

Next row: [K1, p1] 3 times, k2tog, turn (leave rem 17(23:29:35) sts on a stitch holder). *7 sts*

Work k1, p1 rib as set for 6 rows.

Cast off 7 sts.

RS facing, slip sts from stitch holder onto left-hand needle, re-join yarn and cast off until 8 sts remain in total, ssk, [p1, k1] 3 times. *7 sts*

Work k1, p1 rib as set for 6 rows.

Cast off.

FRONT

Cast on 45(51:57:63) sts.

Row 1 (RS): [K1, p1] to last st, k1.

Row 2: [P1, k1] to last st, p1.

Rep rows 1–2, 2(3:3:3) times more.

Next row: [K1, p1] 3 times, k1, work in lace patt to last 7 sts, k1, [p1, k1] 3 times.

Next row: [P1, k1] 3 times, p1, work in lace patt to last 7 sts, p1, [k1, p1] 3 times.

Keeping patt correct as set by last 2 rows, cont until 3(4:5:5) lace patt repeats have been completed.

Shape armholes

Row 1 (RS): Cast off 2 sts (1 st on right-hand needle), [p1, k1] 3 times, k4, work row 1 of lace patt as set to last 7 sts, k1, [p1, k1] 3 times. *43(49:55:61) sts*

Row 2: Cast off 2 sts (1 st on right-hand needle), [k1, p1] 3 times, p4, k1, [p5, k1] to last 11 sts, p5, [k1, p1] 3 times. *41(47:53:59) sts*

Row 3: [K1, p1] 3 times, ssk, p1, k2tog, yo, work row 3 of lace patt as set to last 11 sts, yo, ssk, p1, k2tog, [p1, k1] 3 times. *39(45:51:57) sts*

Row 4: [P1, k1] 3 times, p1, [k1, p5] to last 8 sts, [k1, p1] 4 times.

Row 5: [K1, p1] 3 times, ssk, [k5, p1] to last 13 sts, k5, k2tog, [p1, k1] 3 times. *37(43:49:55) sts*

Row 6: [P1, k1] 3 times, p6, [k1, p5] to last 7 sts, p1, [k1, p1] 3 times.

Row 7: [K1, p1] 3 times, ssk, k1, p1, [k2tog, yo, k1, yo, ssk, p1] to last 9 sts, k1, k2tog, [p1, k1] 3 times. *35(41:47:53) sts*

Row 8: [P1, k1] 3 times, p2, [k1, p5] to last 9 sts, k1, p2, [k1, p1] 3 times.

Row 9: [K1, p1] 3 times, ssk, work row 1 of lace patt as set to last 9 sts, p1, k2tog, [p1, k1] 3 times. *33(39:45:51) sts*

Row 10: [P1, k1] 3 times, p1, k1, [p5, k1] to last 7 sts, p1, [k1, p1] 3 times.

Row 11: [K1, p1] 3 times, ssk, [yo, ssk, p1, k2tog, yo, k1] to last 13 sts, yo, ssk, p1, k2tog, yo, k2tog, [p1, k1] 3 times. *31(37:43:49) sts*

Row 12: [P1, k1] 3 times, p3, [k1, p5] to last 10 sts, k1, p3, [k1, p1] 3 times.

Row 13: [K1, p1] 3 times, ssk, k1, [p1, k5] to last 10 sts, p1, k1, k2tog, [p1, k1] 3 times. *29(35:41:47) sts*

Row 14: [P1, k1] 3 times, p2, [k1, p5] to last 9 sts, k1, p2, [k1, p1] 3 times.

Row 15: [K1, p1] 3 times, ssk, [k1, yo, ssk, p1, k2tog, yo] to last 9 sts, k1, k2tog, [p1, k1] 3 times. *27(33:39:45) sts*

Row 16: [P1, k1] 3 times, p4, [k1, p5] to last 11 sts, k1, p4, [k1, p1] 3 times.

Row 17: [K1, p1] 3 times, ssk, p1, [k1, p1] to last 8 sts, k2tog, [p1, k1] 3 times. *25(31:37:43) sts*

Row 18: [P1, k1] to last st, k1.

Work k1, p1 rib as set for 6(10:10:10) rows.

Shape neckline and straps

Next row: [K1, p1] 3 times, k2tog, turn (leave rem 17(23:29:35) sts on a stitch holder). *7 sts*

Work k1, p1 rib as set for 6 rows.

Cast off 7 sts.

RS facing, slip sts from stitch holder onto left-hand needle, re-join yarn and cast off until 8 sts remain in total, ssk, [p1, k1] 3 times. *7 sts*

Work k1, p1 rib as set for 6 rows.

Cast off.

Weave in loose ends.

Press the pieces following directions on the ball band.

Sew the shoulder straps together, then the side seams.

Lace Vest

Warm Vest

The sleeveless version of this vest works for both boys and girls, but you may wish to add the little cap sleeves for a more feminine touch for girls. The vest can be worn with the button at the front or back as preferred.

MEASUREMENTS

Size	3–6 mths	6–9 mths	9–12 mths	12–18 mths	18–24 mths
Finished chest measurement	44cm	48cm	53cm	57cm	62cm

YARN

1 (1:1:1:2) x 100g skein of Malabrigo Merino Worsted in Simply Taupe 601 or Polar Morn 9

MATERIALS

Pair each of 3.5mm and 4.5mm knitting needles
2 stitch holders
Tapestry needle
Crochet hook
1 x 12mm button
Sewing needle and thread

TENSION

18 sts and 22 rows to 10cm over patt using 4.5mm needles

LPC – slip next 3 sts onto right-hand needle, lift 3 wrapped sts and drop yarnovers to make 3 long sts, keeping them on left-hand needle. Return 3 slipped sts to left-hand needle. Pass 3 long sts over 3 slipped sts, knitting into back of long sts as you go along, then knit the 3 slipped sts. See also page 140

BACK

Using 3.5mm needles, cast on 40(44:48:52:56) sts.
Row 1 (RS): K1(2:3:1:2), [p1, k2] to end of row.
Row 2: [P2, k1] to last 1(2:3:1:2) sts, p1(2:3:1:2).
Rep rows 1–2 twice more.
Change to 4.5mm needles.
Row 7: Knit.
Row 8: Purl.
Row 9: Knit.
Row 10: P2(1:3:2:1), [p3 wrapping yarn over needle twice for each st, p3] to last 2(1:3:2:1) sts, p2(1:3:2:1).
Row 11: K2(1:3:2:1), [LPC] to last 2(1:3:2:1) sts, k2(1:3:2:1).
Row 12: Purl.
Row 13: Knit.
Row 14: Purl.
Row 15: Knit.

Row 16: P5(4:6:5:4), [p3 wrapping yarn over needle twice for each st, p3] to last 5(4:6:5:4) sts, p5(4:6:5:4).

Row 17: K5(4:6:5:4), [LPC] to last 5(4:6:5:4) sts, k5(4:6:5:4).

Row 18: Purl.

Rep rows 7–18, 1(1:1:2:2) times more.

Rep rows 7–12 once more for size 9–12 only.

Shape armholes

Keeping patt correct as set, cast off 1(2:2:3:2) sts at beg of next 2 rows. *38(40:44:46:52) sts*

Next row: Knit, dec 0(1:0:1:1) sts at each end of row. *38(38:44:44:50) sts*

Keeping patt correct as set, work 17 rows.

Shape neckline and straps

Change to 3.5mm needles.*

Next row: K2, [p1, k2] to end of row.

Next row: P2, [k1, p2] to end of row.

Rep last 2 rows, 3 times more.

Next row: K2, p1, k2, turn (leave rem 33(33:39:39:45) sts on a stitch holder). *5 sts*

Next row: P2, k1, p2.

Next row: K2, p1, k2.

Cast off 5 sts.

RS facing, slip sts from stitch holder onto left-hand needle, re-join yarn and cast off until 5 sts remain in total, k2, p1, k2.

Next row: P2, k1, p2.

Next row: K2, p1, k2.

Cast off.

Warm Vest

FRONT

Work as for Back to *.
Next row (RS): K2, [p1, k2] 5(5:6:6:7) times, p1, k1, turn (leave rem 19(19:22:22:25) sts on a stitch holder). *19(19:22:22:25) sts*
Next row: P1, [k1, p2] to end of row.
Rep last 2 rows, 3 times more.
Next row: K2, p1, k2, turn (leave rem 14(14:17:17:20) sts on a second stitch holder). *5 sts*
Next row: P2, k1, p2.
Next row: K2, p1, k2.
Cast off 5 sts.
RS facing, slip sts from second stitch holder onto left-hand needle, re-join yarn and cast off all 14 (14:17:17:20) sts.
RS facing, slip sts from first stitch holder onto left-hand needle and re-join yarn. *19(19:22:22:25) sts*
Next row: K1, [p1, k2] to end of row.
Next row: [P2, k1] to last st, p1.
Rep last 2 rows, 3 times more.
Next row: Cast off until 5 sts remain in total, k2, p1, k1.
Next row: P2, k1, p2.
Next row: K2, p1, k2.
Cast off.

SLEEVE FOR GIRLS (MAKE TWO)

Using 3.5mm needles, cast on 35(35:35:41:41) sts.
Row 1 (RS): K2, [p1, k2] to end of row.
Row 2: P2, [k1, p2] to end of row.
Keeping rib patt correct as set, dec 1 st at each end of next and every alt row for 9 rows. *25(25:25:31:31) sts*
Row 12: Cast off 5(5:5:7:7) sts, k2tog and cast off twice, k3tog and cast off 2(2:2:3:3) times, k2tog and cast off twice, cast off rem sts.

TO MAKE UP

Weave in loose ends.
Press the pieces following directions on the ball band.
Sew the shoulder straps together, then the side seams.
If your vest has sleeves, pin cast-off edge of sleeve evenly around upper edge of armhole, making sure that centre of sleeve is aligned with shoulder strap seam, then sew together.
Crochet a small chain loop for a buttonhole on one side of the centre front neckline. Sew a button on the other side to match.

Warm Vest

Cable Vest

This vest is designed to suit both girls and boys. It is a matter of taste, but if you find the buttoned front to be a bit too feminine for a boy, then simply make two backs for a boy's vest.

MEASUREMENTS

Size	3–6 mths	6–9 mths	9–12 mths	12–18 mths	18–24 mths
Finished chest measurement	41cm	48cm	55cm	61cm	68cm

YARN

2 x 50g balls of Rowan Baby Merino Silk DK in Rose 678 or Zinc 681

MATERIALS

Pair of 3.5mm knitting needles
Cable needle
2 stitch holders
Tapestry needle
Crochet hook
1 x 12mm button
Sewing needle and thread

TENSION

24 sts and 32 rows to 10cm over cable patt using 3.5mm needles

C6B – slip next 4 sts onto cable needle and hold at back of work, knit next 2 sts from left-hand needle, slip the 2 purl sts from cable needle back onto left-hand needle and purl them, then knit 2 sts from cable needle.

C6F – slip next 4 sts onto cable needle and hold at front of work, knit next 2 sts from left-hand needle, slip the 2 purl sts from cable needle back onto left-hand needle and purl them, then knit 2 sts from cable needle.

C6Btog – slip next 4 sts onto cable needle and hold at back of work, purl next 2 sts together from left-hand needle, slip the 2 purl sts from cable needle back onto left-hand needle and purl them, then knit 2 sts from cable needle.

C6Ftog – slip next 4 sts onto cable needle and hold at front of work, knit next 2 sts from left-hand needle, slip the 2 purl sts from cable needle back onto left-hand needle and purl them, then purl 2 sts together from cable needle.

See also page 140

Back

Cast on 50(58:66:74:82) sts.
Row 1 (RS): [P2, k2] to last 2 sts, p2.
Row 2: [K2, p2] to last 2 sts, k2.

Cable Vest

Rep rows 1–2, 3 times more.

Row 9: P2, k2, p2, [C6B, p2] to last 4 sts, k2, p2.

Row 10: [K2, p2] to last 2 sts, k2.

Row 11: [P2, k2] to last 2 sts, p2.

Row 12: [K2, p2] to last 2 sts, k2.

Rep rows 11–12 twice more.

Row 17: [P2, k2] twice, p2, [C6F, p2] to last 8 sts, [k2, p2] twice.

Row 18: [K2, p2] to last 2 sts, k2.

Row 19: [P2, k2] to last 2 sts, p2

Row 20: [K2, p2] to last 2 sts, k2.

Rows 21–24: Rep rows 19–20 twice more.

Rep rows 9–24, 1(1:1:2:2) times more.

Next row: P2, k2, p2, C6Btog, p2, [C6B, p2] to last 12 sts, C6Ftog, p2, k2, p2. *48(56:64:72:80) sts*

Next and all WS rows: Purl the knit sts and knit the purl sts of previous row.

Shape armholes

Keeping patt correct as set, cast off 4 sts at beg of next 2 rows. *40(48:56:64:72) sts*

Dec 1 st at each end of next and every alt row for 6 rows (the last dec row should be a C6F cable row). *34(42:50:58:66) sts*

Patt 8 rows.*

Cont in patt as set for 4(4:12:12:12) rows.

Shape neckline and straps

Now cont in k2, p2 rib as set.

Work 10 sts, turn (leave rem 24(32:40:48:56) sts on a stitch holder).

Work 6 rows.

Cast off 10 sts.
RS facing, slip sts from stitch holder onto left-hand needle, re-join yarn and cast off until 10 sts remain in total, work in rib patt to end.
Work 6 rows.
Cast off.

FRONT

Work as for Back to *.
Cont in patt as set for 0(0:8:8:8) rows.
Shape neckline and straps
Now cont in k2, p2 rib as set.
Work 17(21:25:29:33) sts, turn (leave rem 17(21:25:29:33) sts on a stitch holder).
Work 3 rows.
Work 10 sts, turn (leave rem 7(11:15:19:23) sts on a second stitch holder).
Work 6 rows.
Cast off 10 sts.
RS facing, slip sts from second stitch holder onto left-hand needle, re-join yarn and cast off all sts.
RS facing, slip sts from first stitch holder onto left-hand needle and re-join yarn. *17(21:25:29:33) sts*
Work 4 rows.
Cast off 7(11:15:19:23) sts and work in rib patt to end. *(10 sts)*
Work 6 rows.
Cast off.

TO MAKE UP

Weave in loose ends.
Steam the pieces following directions on the ball band.
Sew the shoulder straps together, then the side seams.
Crochet a small chain loop for a buttonhole on one side of the centre front neckline. Sew a button on the other side to match.

Cable Vest

Accessories

Hat with Wave

The wavy pattern in this hat works well for covering up the forehead and keeping warm.

MEASUREMENTS

Size	pre–0 mths	0–3 mths	3–6 mths	6–9 mths
Finished head measurement	29cm	31cm	33.5cm	38cm

YARN

1 x 50g ball of Rowan Wool Cotton in Smalt 963

MATERIALS

Pair of 3.5mm knitting needles
Tapestry needle

TENSION

18 sts and 34 rows to 10cm over garter stitch using 3.5mm needles

ABBREVIATIONS

See page 140

Hat

Cast on 55(59:63:71) sts.
Rows 1–2: Knit.
Row 3 (RS): [K1, p1] 4 times, k1, yo,
k10(12:14:18), yo, [k1, p1] 8 times, k1, yo,
k10(12:14:18), yo, [k1, p1] 4 times, k1.
59(63:67:75) sts
Row 4: [P1, k1] 4 times, p2, k10(12:14:18), p2,
[k1, p1] 8 times, p1, k10(12:14:18), p2, [k1, p1]
4 times.
Row 5: [K1, p1] 4 times, k1, yo, k12(14:16:20), yo,
[k1, p1] 8 times, k1, yo, k12(14:16:20), yo, [k1, p1]
4 times, k1. *63(67:71:79) sts*
Row 6: [P1, k1] 4 times, p2, k12(14:16:20), p2,
[k1, p1] 8 times, p1, k12(14:16:20), p2, [k1, p1]
4 times.
Row 7: [K1, p1] 4 times, k1, yo, k14(16:18:22), yo,
[k1, p1] 8 times, k1, yo, k14(16:18:22), yo, [k1, p1]
4 times, k1. *67(71:75:83) sts*
Row 8: [P1, k1] 4 times, p2, k14(16:18:22), p2,
[k1, p1] 8 times, p1, k14(16:18:22), p2, [k1, p1]
4 times.
Row 9: [K1, p1] 4 times, k1, yo, k16(18:20:24), yo,
[k1, p1] 8 times, k1, yo, k16(18:20:24), yo, [k1, p1]
4 times, k1. *71(75:79:87) sts*
Row 10: [P1, k1] 4 times, p2, k16(18:20:24), p2,
[k1, p1] 8 times, p1, k16(18:20:24), p2, [k1, p1]
4 times.

Row 11: K1, [k2tog] 4 times, k19(21:23:27),
[k2tog] 8 times, k19(21:23:27), [k2tog] 4 times.
55(59:63:71) sts
Row 12: Knit.
Rep rows 3–12, 1(1:1:2) times more, then rep
rows 3–10 once more. *71(75:79:87) sts*
Next row: K1, [k4tog] twice, k1, [k4tog] 4(4:5:6)
times, [k2tog] 0(1:0:0) times, k2, [k4tog] 4 times,
k1, [k4tog] 4(4:5:6) times, [k2tog] 0(1:0:0) times,
k2, [k4tog] twice. *23(25:25:27) sts*
Cast off.

To make up

Weave in loose ends.
Press the piece following directions on the
ball band.
Sew the row ends together, then fold the hat in
half with seam at centre and sew the top seam.

Hat with Wave

Stay-on Ribbed Boots

A little pair of baby boots for tiny feet.

MEASUREMENTS

Size	0–3 mths
Finished sole measurement	9cm

YARN

1 x 50g ball of Rowan Pima Cotton DK in Lozenge 055

MATERIALS

Pair of 3mm knitting needles
Tapestry needle
Approx 25 x 25cm of lambskin and strong sewing needle and thread for soles
(optional)

TENSION

20 sts and 28 rows to 10cm over st st using 3mm needles

ABBREVIATIONS

See page 140

Upper (make two)

Cast on 57 sts.
Row 1 (RS): Knit.
Row 2: [P1, k1] to last st, p1.
Row 3: [K1, p1] to last st, k1.
Row 4: [P1, k1] to last st, p1.
Rep rows 3–4 twice more.
Row 9: [K1, p1] 10 times, [ssk] 4 times, k1, [k2tog] 4 times, [p1, k1] 10 times. 49 sts
Row 10: [P1, k1] 10 times, [p2tog] twice, p1, [p2tog] twice, [k1, p1] 10 times. 45 sts
Row 11: [K1, p1] 10 times, ssk, k1, k2tog, [p1, k1] 10 times. 43 sts
Row 12: [P1, k1] 9 times, [p1, p2tog] twice, p1, [k1, p1] 9 times. 41 sts
Row 13: [K1, p1] 9 times, ssk, k1, k2tog, [p1, k1] 9 times. 39 sts
Row 14: [P1, k1] 8 times, [p1, p2tog] twice, p1, [k1, p1] 8 times. 37 sts
Row 15: [K1, p1] 8 times, ssk, k1, k2tog, [p1, k1] 8 times. 35 sts
Row 16: [P1, k1] 7 times, [p1, p2tog] twice, p1, [k1, p1] 7 times. 33 sts
Row 17: [K1, p1] 7 times, ssk, k1, k2tog, [p1, k1] 7 times. 31 sts
Row 18: [P1, k1] 6 times, [p1, p2tog] twice, p1, [k1, p1] 6 times. 29 sts
Row 19: [K1, p1] 6 times, ssk, k1, k2tog, [p1, k1] 6 times. 27 sts
Row 20: [P1, k1] 5 times, [p1, p2tog] twice, p1, [k1, p1] 5 times. 25 sts
Row 21: [K1, p1] 5 times, ssk, k1, k2tog, [p1, k1] 5 times. 23 sts
Row 22: [P1, k1] 5 times, p3, [k1, p1] 5 times.
Row 23: [K1, p1] 5 times, k3, [p1, k1] 5 times.
Row 24: [P1, k1] 5 times, p3, [k1, p1] 5 times.
Rep rows 23–24 twice more, then rep row 23 once more.
Cast off.

Sole (make two)

Cast on 7 sts.
Row 1 (RS): Knit.
Row 2: Purl.
Rep rows 1–2 once more.
Row 5: K2, inc 1, k1, inc 1, k2. 9 sts
Row 6: Purl.
Row 7: Knit.
Row 8: Purl.
Row 9: K2, inc 1, k3, inc 1, k2. 11 sts
Row 10: Purl.
Work 6 rows st st.
Row 17: K2, ssk, k3, k2tog, k2. 9 sts
Row 18: Purl.
Row 19: Knit.
Row 20: Purl.
Row 21: K2, ssk, k1, k2tog, k2. 7 sts

Stay-on Ribbed Boots

Row 22: Purl.
Row 23: Knit.
Row 24: Purl.
For a single-layer sole, cast off.
For a double-layer sole, rep rows 1–23 once more
and then cast off.

TO MAKE UP

Weave in loose ends
Press the pieces following directions on the
ball band.
For each boot, sew the upper piece together to
form seam at back of ankle. Fold the 8 rows of rib
at top of ankle in half towards the inside and slip
stitch the cast-off edge in place.
If using a double-layer sole, fold it WS together.
Pin the upper to the sole, making sure that it is
positioned evenly, then sew together.
For extra comfort, you may wish to cut out a piece
of lambskin the same shape as the sole and sew it
to the bottom of the boot.

Lace Blanket in Merino Wool

The pattern for this blanket has an odd number of rows which makes it reversible. Once you get going you will see how easy it is – as long as you keep track of your stitch counting.

MEASUREMENTS

Size	one size
Finished measurements	54 x 58cm

YARN

3 x 50g balls of MillaMia Naturally Soft Merino in Fawn 160

MATERIALS

Pair each of 2.5mm and 3.5mm knitting needles
Tapestry needle

TENSION

22 sts and 26 rows to 10cm over patt using 3.5mm needles

ABBREVIATIONS

See page 140

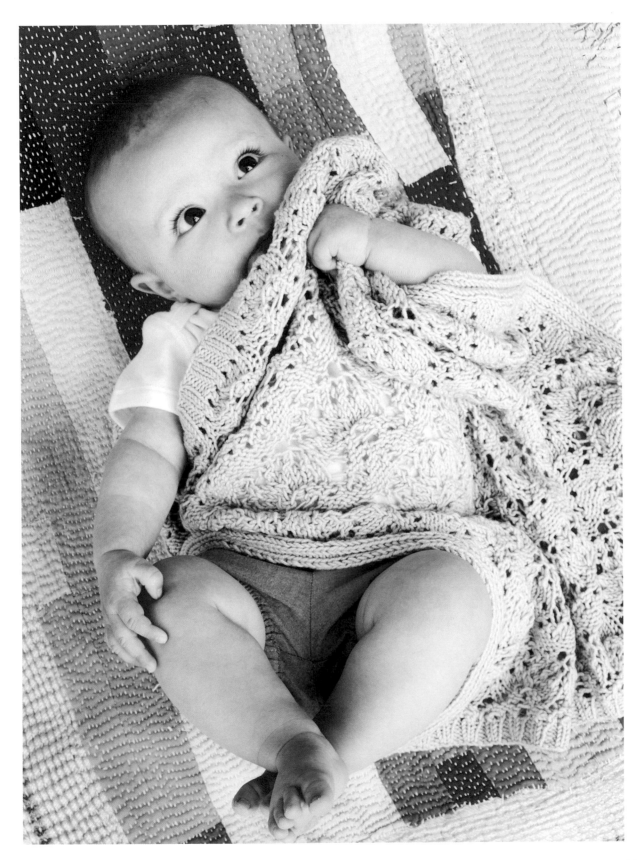

BLANKET

Using 2.5mm needles, cast on 122 sts.
Row 1: K2, [p2, k2] to end of row.
Row 2: P2, [k2, p2] to end of row.
Rep rows 1–2 twice more.
Change to 3.5mm needles.
Row 7: K2, p2, k2, [yo, k2tog] to last 6 sts, k2, p2, k2.
Row 8: P2, k2, p to last 4 sts, k2, p2.
Row 9: K2, p2, k to last 4 sts, p2, k2.
Row 10: P2, k2, p to last 4 sts, k2, p2.
Row 11: K2, p2, k2, [sk2po, k4, yo, k1, yo, k4] to last 6 sts, k2, p2, k2.
Row 12: P2, k2, p2, [p3tog, p4, yo, p1, yo, p4] to last 6 sts, p2, k2, p2.
Row 13: K2, p2, k2, [p3tog, p4, yo, p1, yo, p4] to last 6 sts, k2, p2, k2.
Row 14: P2, k2, p2, [sk2po, k4, yo, k1, yo, k4] to last 6 sts, p2, k2, p2.
Row 15: K2, p2, k2, [p3tog, p4, yo, p1, yo, p4] to last 6 sts, k2, p2, k2.
Row 16: P2, k2, p2, [yo, k2tog] to last 6 sts, p2, k2, p2.
Row 17: K2, p2, k2, p to last 6 sts, k2, p2, k2.
Row 18: P2, k2, p2, k to last 6 sts, p2, k2, p2.
Row 19: K2, p2, k2, p to last 6 sts, k2, p2, k2.
Row 20: P2, k2, p2, [sk2po, k4, yo, k1, yo, k4] to last 6 sts, p2, k2, p2.
Row 21: K2, p2, k2, [p3tog, p4, yo, p1, yo, p4] to last 6 sts, k2, p2, k2.
Row 22: P2, k2, p2, [p3tog, p4, yo, p1, yo, p4] to last 6 sts, p2, k2, p2.
Row 23: K2, p2, k2, [sk2po, k4, yo, k1, yo, k4] to last 6 sts, k2, p2, k2.
Row 24: P2, k2, p2, [p3tog, p4, yo, p1, yo, p4] to last 6 sts, p2, k2, p2.
Rep rows 7–24, 6 times more, then rep rows 7–16 once more.
Change to 2.5mm needles.
Next row: K2, [p2, k2] to end of row.
Next row: P2, [k2, p2] to end of row.
Rep last 2 rows twice more.
Cast off.

TO MAKE UP

Weave in loose ends.
Steam the blanket following directions on the ball band.

Lace Blanket in Merino Wool

Lace Blanket in Linen and Cotton

Perfect for both boys and girls, this lacy blanket worked in a lovely linen and cotton yarn is ideal for summer days. The yarn has a few tiny hairs in it, so do use a different kind if you wish to avoid this.

MEASUREMENTS

Size   one size
Finished measurements   65 x 72cm

YARN

2 x 100g skeins of Rowan Creative Linen in Salmon 627

MATERIALS

Pair of 4mm knitting needles
Tapestry needle

TENSION

14 sts and 23 rows to 10cm over patt using 4mm needles

ABBREVIATIONS

See page 140

BLANKET

Cast on 91 sts.

Starting with a k row, work 11 rows st st.

Row 12 (WS): P8, k3, [p3, k3] 12 times, p8.

Row 13: K8, p1, yo, p2tog, [k3, p1, yo, p2tog] 12 times, k8.

Row 14: P8, k3, [p3, k3] 12 times, p8.

Row 15: K8, p2tog, yo, p1, [k3, p2tog, yo, p1] 12 times, k8.

Row 16: P8, k3, [p3, k3] 12 times, p8.

Row 17: K8, p2, yo, p1, [sk2po, (p1, yo) twice, p1] to last 14 sts, sk2po, p1, yo, p2, k8.

Row 18: P11, [k3, p3] 12 times, p8.

Row 19: K11, [p2tog, yo, p1, k3] 12 times, k8.

Row 20: P11, [k3, p3] 12 times, p8.

Row 21: K11, [p1, yo, p2tog, k3] 12 times, k8.

Row 22: P11, [k3, p3] 12 times, p8.

Row 23: K9, k2tog, [(p1, yo) twice, p1, sk2po] to last 14 sts, [p1, yo] twice, p1, ssk, k9.

Rep rows 12–23, 11 times more, then rep rows 12–14 once more.

Work 10 rows st st.

Cast off.

TO MAKE UP

Weave in loose ends.

Steam the blanket following directions on the ball band.

Lace Blanket in Linen and Cotton

Little Dolphin Sleeping Bag

This might be more for fun than for practicality! It was designed as a warming sleeping bag for newborns.

MEASUREMENTS

Size	0–5 mths
Finished 'waist' measurement	50cm
Finished length measurement	40cm

YARN

3 x 50g balls of MillaMia Naturally Soft Merino in Storm 102

MATERIALS

Pair each of 2.75mm and 3.5mm knitting needles
Cable needle
Stitch holder
Tapestry needle
Approx 1m of 1.5cm ribbon to tie (optional)
Safety pin or bodkin

TENSION

30 sts and 30 rows to 10cm over cable patt using 3.5mm needles

C4B – slip next 2 sts onto cable needle and hold at back of work, knit next 2 sts from left-hand needle, then knit 2 sts from cable needle.
C4F – slip next 2 sts onto cable needle and hold at front of work, knit next 2 sts from left-hand needle, then knit 2 sts from cable needle.
See also page 140

DOLPHIN BODY (MAKE TWO)

Using 2.75mm needles, cast on 74 sts.
Row 1 (RS): [K1, p1] to end of row.
Rep row 1, 13 times more.
Change to 3.5mm needles.
Row 15: Knit.
Row 16 and all WS rows: Purl.
Row 17: K1, [C4B, C4F] to last st, k1.
Row 19: Knit.
Row 21: K1, [C4F, C4B] to last st, k1.
Row 23: Knit.
Row 24: Purl.
Rep rows 17–24 twice more, then rep rows 17–21 once more.
Next row: Purl, dec 1 st at each end of row. *72 sts*
Keeping cable patt correct as set, dec 1 st at each end of next and every alt row until there are 34 sts.
Patt 7 rows.
Cont in patt, inc 1 st at each end of every row until there are 66 sts.

Divide for 'feet'

Next row (RS): K2, m1, k27, k2tog, k2, turn (leave rem 33 sts on a stitch holder). *33 sts*

Next row: P31, m1, p2. *34 sts*

Next row: Work cable patt as set, inc 1 st at beg and dec 1 st at end of row as set. *34 sts*

Next row: P32, m1, p2. *35 sts*

Next row: Work patt as set, inc 1 st at beg and dec 1 st at end of row as set. *35 sts*

Next row: P to last 2 sts, m1, p2. *36 sts*

Rep last 2 rows once more. *37 sts*

Next row: Work patt as set, inc 1 st at beg and dec 1 st at end of row as set. *37 sts*

Next row: P2, p2tog, p to end of row. *36 sts*

Rep last 2 rows twice more. *34 sts*

Next row: Work patt as set to last 4 sts, k2tog, k2. *33 sts*

Next row: P2, p2tog, p to end of row. *32 sts*

Rep last 2 rows, 3 times more. *26 sts*

Next row: Work patt as set.

Cast off, knitting 2 sts together each time before passing over.

Working second 'foot'

RS facing, slip sts from stitch holder onto needle and re-join yarn.

Next row (RS): K2, ssk, k27, m1, k2. *33 sts*

Next row: P2, m1, p31. *34 sts*

Next row: Work cable patt as set, inc 1 st at beg and dec 1 st at end of row as set. *34 sts*

Next row: P2, m1, p32. *35 sts*

Next row: Work patt as set, dec 1 st at beg and inc 1 st at end of row as set. *35 sts*

Next row: P2, m1, p to end of row. *36 sts*

Rep last 2 rows once more. *37 sts*

Next row: Work patt as set, dec 1 st at beg and inc 1 st at end of row as set. *37 sts*

Next row: P to last 4 sts, p2tog, p2. *36 sts*

Rep last 2 rows twice more. *34 sts*

Next row: K2, ssk, patt to end of row. *33 sts*

Next row: P to last 4 sts, p2tog, p2. *32 sts*

Rep last 2 rows, 3 times more. *26 sts*

Next row: Work patt as set.

Cast off, knitting 2 sts together each time before passing over.

To make up

Weave in loose ends.

Press the pieces following directions on the ball band.

Lay the pieces on top of each other, WS together, and sew around the sides and feet, leaving the rib section at the top of one side open.

Fold the rib in half towards the inside and slip stitch the cast-on edge in place to make a channel for the ribbon. Using a safety pin or bodkin, slip the ribbon through the channel and tie at the side, making sure to trim the ribbon so that no excess remains.

Little Dolphin Sleeping Bag

Lace Scarf for Mum

A little luxury for mum or a lovely present for a good
friend. I could not resist making this shawl in a beautiful
lace yarn made in alpaca.

MEASUREMENTS

Size   one size
Finished measurements   41.5 x 143cm

YARN

3 x 50g balls of Rowan Fine Lace in Cobweb 922 used DOUBLE throughout

MATERIALS

Pair of 4mm knitting needles
Tapestry needle

TENSION

18 sts and 30 rows to 10cm over st st using 4mm needles and two strands of
yarn held together

ABBREVIATIONS

See page 140

Note: You can make the scarf a bit longer if you prefer, but remember that you
may need more yarn.

Main section

Using 2 strands of yarn, cast on 75 sts.
Row 1 (RS): Knit.
Row 2: Purl.
Row 3: Knit.
Row 4: P3, [k3, p3] to end of row.
Row 5: K3, [p2tog, yo, p1, k3] to end of row.
Row 6: As row 4.
Row 7: K3, [p1, yo, p2tog, k3] to end of row.
Row 8: As row 4.
Row 9: K1, k2tog, [(p1, yo) twice, p1, sk2po]
11 times, [p1, yo] twice, p1, ssk, k1.
Row 10: K3, [p3, k3] to end of row.
Row 11: P1, yo, p2tog, [k3, p1, yo, p2tog] to end
of row.
Row 12: As row 10.
Row 13: P2tog, yo, p1, [k3, p2tog, yo, p1] to end
of row.
Row 14: As row 10.
Row 15: P2, yo, p1, [sk2po, (p1, yo) twice, p1]
11 times, sk2po, p1, yo, p2.
Rep rows 4–15, 3 times more.
Starting with a p row, work 10cm in st st, ending
with a RS row.
*Rep rows 4–15, 4 times more.
Starting with a p row, work 10cm in st st, ending
with a RS row.
Rep from * twice more.
Rep rows 4–15, 4 times more.
Knit 1 row.
Cast off.

Lace edge (make two)

Using 2 strands of yarn, cast on 9 sts.
Row 1 (RS): Knit.
Row 2: Purl.
Row 3: Sl 1, k1, yo, k2tog, [yo, k1] 3 times, yo,
k2. *13 sts*
Row 4: P11, k2.
Row 5: Sl 1, k1, yo, k2tog, yo, k3, yo, k1, yo, k3,
yo, k2. *17 sts*
Row 6: P15, k2.
Row 7: Sl 1, k1, yo, k2tog, yo, sl 2, k3tog, p2sso,
yo, k1, yo, sl 2, k3tog, p2sso, yo, k2. *13 sts*
Row 8: Cast off 4 sts (1 st on right-hand needle),
p6, k2. *9 sts*
Rep rows 3–8 until edge equals width of scarf.
Cast off.

To make up

Weave in loose ends.
Steam the pieces following directions on the
all band.
Sew a lace edge to each end of the main section.

Lace Scarf for Mum

Abbreviations

alt	alternate; alternatively	p	purl
approx	approximately	p2tog	purl two stitches (or number stated) together
beg	begin(s)(ning)		
C4B	cable four stitches (or number stated) back	patt(s)	pattern(s)
		psso	pass slipped stitch over
C4F	cable four stitches (or number stated) front	p2sso	pass two slipped stitches over
		rem	remain(ing)
cm	centimetre(s)	rep	repeat
cont	continue(ing)	RS	right side
dec	decrease(s)(ing)	sk2po	slip one stitch, knit two stitches together, pass slipped stitch over
DK	double knit		
foll(s)	follow(s)(ing)	sl	slip
g	gram	ssk	slip one stitch, slip one stitch, knit slipped stitches together through the back loops
inc	increase(s)(ing)		
inc 1	work into front and back of same stitch to increase by one stitch		
		st st	stocking stitch
k	knit	st(s)	stitch(es)
k2tog	knit two stitches (or number stated) together	tog	together
		WS	wrong side
LPC	left purl cross	wyib	with yarn in back
m1	make one stitch by lifting strand between needles and working into back of it	wyif	with yarn in front
		yo	yarn over needle
		*	repeat instruction after/between * as many times as stated
MB	make bobble		
MK	make knot	[ ]	repeat instruction between [ ] as many times as stated
mm	millimetre(s)		
mth(s)	month(s)		

Choosing Yarn

If you are buying the yarn recommended in the pattern you have chosen to knit, then you just have to choose the colour you want. However, if you are substituting a recommended pattern yarn for another yarn, then there are some rules to follow.

First, unless you are practised at altering patterns, choose a substitute yarn that is the same weight as the pattern yarn – trying to knit an Aran-weight pattern with a 4-ply yarn will create huge problems. Even if you have chosen a substitute yarn that is the recommended weight, be aware that yarns of the same weight do not always knit up to the same tension, so you must work a tension swatch. The ball band of the substitute yarn will provide an average tension, and as long as this doesn't differ by more than one stitch from that of the pattern yarn, you should be able to achieve the right tension by changing needle size. More than one stitch difference could cause problems.

Then you have to work out how much of the substitute yarn you need. You cannot simply buy the number of balls stated in the pattern because, even though the balls may weigh the same as those of the pattern yarn, they will not necessarily contain the same number of metres of yarn, and it is this that is important. To work out how many balls of substitute yarn you need to buy, you must do the following sum.

Number of metres of yarn in one ball of pattern yarn, multiplied by the number of balls needed, to give you the total number of metres of yarn needed.

Total number of metres needed, divided by the number of metres of yarn in one ball of the substitute yarn, to give you the number of balls of substitute yarn you need to buy.

FOR EXAMPLE

125 metres per ball of the pattern yarn, and 15 balls are needed.
125 x 15 = 1875 metres in total of yarn needed.

95 metres per ball of the substitute yarn.
1875 ÷ by 95 = 19.73.
Therefore you will need to buy 20 balls of the substitute yarn.

If you have a good local yarn shop then the staff should also be able to help you in making a suitable yarn choice.

If you are using a substitute yarn, it is always worth knitting first the back and then one sleeve. This is approximately halfway through a sweater and you will be able to see whether you are going to have enough yarn to finish the project.

Yarn Information

Debbie Bliss Baby Cashmerino: 125m/50g ball: 55% merino wool, 33% microfibre, 12% cashmere.

Debbie Bliss Bella: 95m/50g ball; 85% cotton, 10% silk, 5% cashmere.

Debbie Bliss Eco Aran: 75m/50g ball; 100% organic cotton.

Debbie Bliss Rialto Aran: 80m/50g ball; 100% merino wool.

Malabrigo Merino Worsted: 192m/100g skein; 100% merino wool.

MillaMia Naturally Soft Merino: 125m/50g ball; 100% extra fine merino wool.

Rowan Baby Merino Silk DK: 135m/50g ball; 66% super wash wool, 34% silk.

Rowan Belle Organic DK by Amy Butler:120m/50g ball; 50% organic cotton, 50% organic wool.

Rowan Cashsoft DK: 115m/50g ball; 10% cashmere, 57% extra fine merino wool, 33% acrylic microfibre.

Rowan Creative Linen: 200m/100g skein; 50% linen, 50% cotton.

Rowan Fine Lace: 400m/50g ball; 80% baby suri alpaca, 20% fine merino wool.

Rowan Pima Cotton DK: 130m/50g ball; 100% pima cotton.

Rowan Pure Wool DK: 125m/50g ball; 100% super wash wool.

Rowan Wool Cotton: 113m/50g ball; 50% cotton, 50% merino wool.

Suppliers

Debbie Bliss www.designeryarns.uk.com
Malabrigo www.malabrigoyarn.com
MillaMia www.millamia.com
Rowan www.knitrowan.com

Conversions

NEEDLE SIZES

This table gives you the equivalent sizes across all three systems of sizing needles.

Metric	US	old UK/Canadian
25	50	–
19	35	–
15	19	–
10	15	000
9	13	00
8	11	0
7.5	11	1
7	10½	2
6.5	10½	3
6	10	4
5.5	9	5
5	8	6
4.5	7	7
4	6	8
3.75	5	9
3.5	4	–
3.25	3	10
3	2/3	11
2.75	2	12
2.25	1	13
2	0	14
1.75	00	–
1.5	000	–

WEIGHTS AND LENGTHS

grams = ounces x 28.35
ounces = grams x 0.0352
centimetres = inches x 2.54
inches = centimetres x 0.3937
metres = yards x 1.0936
yards = metres x 0.9144

Acknowledgements

There is no doubt that there are quite a few people without whose help this book would never have come about.

The people at Collins & Brown have all been an immense help. Amy Christian for making sure everything goes to plan and for being understanding and supportive when it doesn't. Laura Russell and the graphic design team for helping me with the photography and making a wonderful layout. Margarita Lygizou for including me in promotion and explaining how it all works.

Michelle Pickering for her first and in-depth pattern checking, which I'm sure must have caused a few grey hairs. Marilyn Wilson for her perseverance, thorough work, patience and support while checking my patterns. Honestly, without their help, there would be no patterns!

Kate Buller, Marie Wallin, David MacLeod, Vicky Sedgwick from Rowan, Katarina Rosen from MillaMia and Dionne Taylor from Designer Yarns who not only provided me with beautiful yarns, but also encouraged my work.

Suzie Zuber, a mom and super-knitter, for her expert advice, ideas and support.

The people at Nest in Crouch End and the staff at John Lewis Oxford Street who always take the time to give advice and ideas.

My little models and their parents: Bella Blu, Nanna, Jasmine, Ottilie, Rahul, Alexander, Iben, Jameelah and Nicolas. Everyone of you have been so incredibly helpful, patient and encouraging.

Antonio who has always supported me in my pursuit of knitting and designing, and who is very generous with his hugs when I need it.

My family; my mom who always helps when there is something I'm not sure how to do, my dad for updating me on everything about my book in Denmark, my sister, Martin and my nephew and niece for testing out my clothes, Birthe for more or less buying half of all the US copies of my first book, my nan who passed away this year but would have made an excellent PR agent, and so many more...

My friends for their words of encouragement and interest.

About the Author

Vibe Ulrik Sondergaard studied fashion design at Kingston University, London, (2004–2007) and also at the Brooks Institute of Photography, Santa Barbara, California (2001–2002).

Vibe currently works for Zinc Design Ltd, designing and producing hand-knitted swatches that are sold to fashion companies in New York, LA, Paris, Barcelona and London. Design credits include Nicole Farhi and Whistles. Vibe's colourful, textured designs are both practical and beautiful.

Picture Credits

Cover photography and pages 5, 58, 63, 102 & 105 by Rachel Whiting.

All other photography by Vibe Ulrik Sondergaard.

The Provenza paper (used as a background) is made in Italy by Grafiche Tassotti ©.

Whatever the craft, we have the book for you – just head straight to Collins & Brown crafty HeadQuarters!

LoveCrafts is the one-stop destination for all things crafty, with the very latest news and information about all our books and authors. It doesn't stop there...

Enter our fabulous competitions and win great prizes
Download free patterns from our talented authors
Collect LoveCrafts loyalty points and receive special offers on all our books

Join our crafting community at LoveCrafts – we look forward to meeting you!

From the same author

Labour of Love, £16.99
978-1-84340-633-4

This beautiful book of functional, stylish designs for little girls contains over 20 unique knitting patterns for sweaters, cardigans, dresses and tops, skirts and snoods and charming accessories.

Combining true comfort with contemporary design, in a world where time is precious and clothes are often mass-produced, Danish knitwear designer Vibe Ulrik Sondergaard has produced a delightful range of garments that are definitely worth investing time into. Many of the designs focus on texture and shape in solid colours, and all aim to be functional for active children. They are feminine but not too childish in look and feel.

Beautiful stitches, quirky details, classic shapes and lush yarns are combined to inspire others to create their own 'Labour of Love'.